Praise

'I came across this programme as a delegate where it touched my heart and stimulated my mind so much that I knew it had to be shared. I was delighted when the book came to print and was one of the first to become accredited to deliver it.'
— **Suzanne Jones**, Practitioner

'An outstanding aid to delivering real improvements in performance.'
— **Paul Birch**, MBA BA ACII, Therapy and Coaching

'It's theory that when put into practice really does make a significant difference when you are leading a business.'
— **Andy Steele**, CEO, Stephens Scown Solicitors, www.stephens-scown.co.uk

'If you are searching for some magic keys to unlock people potential, this book is an ideal read. We find Ali & Derek's accessible models and language invaluable elements for our leadership and management development work.'
— **Sally Foan**, retired founder of People Tree Training

'As an engineer, twenty years of management have gone by thinking about systems, machinery, investment, budgets, etc. Only now have I discovered how to oil, tune, grease and maintain the biggest resource... humans. Thanks to Ali and Derek.'
— **Muzaffer Erdal Kilic**, BSc Nav Arch M Mech Eng, General Manager

'Organisations have the capacity to stultify or to liberate. *The Liberator* is a manual for building the human skills necessary to unleash our own performance to build high-performing teams and to guide organisational transformation.'
— **Deepak Rughani**, MSc, Environmental Campaigning and Sustainable Living

'I have been using the concepts and content of Ali & Derek's book in my work when developing managers and leaders across a broad range of organisations, all with outstanding results. When a top clients says, "this is the most informative management development course I have attended in thirty-five years," you know this is something special.'
— **Peter Johnson**, a leader in developing people and businesses,
www.peterjohnsononline.com

'What I love about *The Liberator* is its simplicity. It is so easy for managers to access and implement, either as a whole programme or for one-off situations – for example

just using the Performance Navigator. It's a practical handbook that helps managers develop into great leaders by helping their teams fulfil their potential.'
   — **Elaine Batt**, Founder of Burner Consulting Ltd

'This is clear, concise and facilitates genuine structured learning.'
   — **Carole Noakes**, Director, Voice Ltd

'The unique selling point of Ali & Derek's book is that it tells managers how to behave to become accepted as leaders. There are lots of books on leadership but very few are so practical and applied.'
   — **Geoff Ribbens**, Author *Body Language* and *Body Language in a Week*

'I first came across *The Liberator* programme while working with an organisation who were so enthused and converted by his process that it made me want to go out and be part of it. Having become accredited through Ali Stewart, I feel like I've got a completely new lease of life as a Management Training Consultant. Between them, they have given me structure, meaning and a much-needed process that has left me inspired, enthused and able to deliver management training that really does have a lasting effect. Best training I've ever embarked on. Thanks.'
   — **Emma Brereton**, The Kudos Group

'For me, *The Liberator* brings together years of teaching and learning around leadership development in one place – a real gem! A very common-sense approach to bringing about real and very sustainable improvements in performance. Based on an understanding of self and own style as a leader, it then cleverly weaves this through the performance management cycle in a way that will help any people manager navigate the process in a rational, straightforward and understandable way.'
— **Paul Thompson**, Owner, Westminster Associates Ltd

Ali Stewart & Co

The Liberator
A transformational approach to leading high performance

Ali Stewart & Dr Derek S Biddle

Re think

This edition published in Great Britain in 2024 by Rethink Press (www.rethinkpress.com)

First published in 2015 under the title *Liberating Leadership*

© Copyright Ali Stewart & Dr Derek S Biddle

All rights reserved. No part of this publication may be reproduced, stored in or introduced into a retrieval system, or transmitted, in any form, or by any means (electronic, mechanical, photocopying, recording or otherwise) without the prior written permission of the publisher.

The right of Ali Stewart and Dr Derek S Biddle to be identified as the author of this work has been asserted by them in accordance with the Copyright, Designs and Patents Act 1988.

This book is sold subject to the condition that it shall not, by way of trade or otherwise, be lent, resold, hired out, or otherwise circulated without the publisher's prior consent in any form of binding or cover other than that in which it is published and without a similar condition including this condition being imposed on the subsequent purchaser.

Cover image © Ali Stewart & Co Ltd

One-line illustrations courtesy of Rob Lee
www.robotoon.com

Contents

Preface	1
Foreword	3
Introduction	5
1. **The Crux**	**9**
Part 1: The Mirror	11
Part 2: The Mindset	25
2. **The Steps: What High-performing Leader-Developers Actually Do**	**65**
The 4-Step Process: Visioning, Mobilising, Developing, Enabling	67
3. **The Skills: Mobilising Step - Under-developed Skills**	**113**
M1: Be Explicit	115
M2: Get to the Root of Issues	129
4. **The Secrets: Mobilising Step - Uncovered**	**165**
M3: Be Appropriately Assertive	167
M4: Give Empowering Feedback	175

5. **The Gear Change: Developing Step - Transformational Leadership** 209
   D1: Know Individual Needs and Motivations 211
   D2: Flexibly Adapt Style 241

6. **The Impact** 267
   The Test: Leading Change and Transition 269
   The Review: Putting It All Together 289

Bibliography 297

Theories Explained 301

Index 325

Other Books In The Series 327

Next Steps 333

The Authors 335

Preface

We first published this book in 2008 under the title *Leading & Developing High Performance*, which was quite a mouthful, and only ever intended as a working title. It summed up the essence of our approach and we couldn't think of anything else that so aptly captured this.

Then, in 2012, I became accredited to use the beautiful Insights Deeper Discovery model, which took you to the heart of Carl Jung's teaching. I was drawn to one of the archetypes in my profile, the Liberator: 'directs us to think for ourselves, breaking free from constraints, and uncovering our untapped potential'. I thought I had it now, by renaming the book *Liberating Leadership*.

With its new name, the book then began opening doors around the world; there was something appealing about the word 'Liberating' that captured the imagination – from Lagos to Dallas, Paramaribo to Amsterdam.

And now, with our 2024 thinking, and the rapidly changing world, we are called on to act differently and think differently. There needs to be fluidity and creativity; and we still need to break free from our own constraints and seek to uncover our untapped potential.

So here comes *The Liberator* in its purest sense. And when we liberate ourselves, we can then liberate others.

The book has a fresh new appeal and is packed with new content, although the essence of our award-winning approach hasn't changed. We still need truly authentic leaders who have a clear vision, who can support and challenge in equal measure, who can motivate and inspire the best in others, so they can achieve more than they ever imagined.

For our existing clients and practitioners, who constantly shine the light, we hope you like the new look. I am grateful to so many for their input into the on-going development of our approach and development of their own clients using the ethos of *The Liberator*.

Together, we have helped our clients win national training awards, turned around teams, saved leaders from burnout and despair. *The Liberator* can help you too, to better manage your relationships, your teams, your organisations. It gives you a beautiful track to run on, leaving nothing to chance.

If you are ready, let's go, enjoy *The Liberator*.

With warmth and best wishes,
Ali

Foreword

The world of business is being turned on its head by the development of technologies that are designed to enhance business performance, measure inputs and outputs, control risk and even reshape job roles, sometimes replacing human interventions with robotic processes. With the demands created by growing transparency it has never been more important to manage well and lead exceptionally.

In the modern business environment it is easy to overlook the role people play in achieving success. Derek Biddle and Ali Stewart have a pedigree in focusing on what people bring to an organisation, especially the business culture that creates the opportunity for individuals at all levels of business to thrive for themselves and for the business they serve.

Derek and Ali long ago recognised that business success is a direct outcome of people engagement. That is, real engagement and empowerment, not simply a vision without implementation. *The Liberator* delivers not only the thinking but the tools and actions that make the difference and deliver the results.

Settle down to a journey that will leave its mark on you. *The Liberator* delivers real value for money. It champions tried and tested methods of leadership in organisations and it is a really good mirror for you to see yourself and change what you see to become the leader you aspire to be.

The Liberator works at all levels; get started...

Paul Walkinshaw, Owner,
Walkinshaw Consulting

Introduction

Derek and I have been working together for over twenty years. This book has evolved from all the research, training, testing and refining we have been doing with our clients over that time, and for Derek the twenty or so years before that.

This means the methodology we are describing is nothing new. But the absolute beauty of it, and where we perhaps see things differently from others, is The Mindset and Process that the highest performing leaders operate to.

Leadership is a process and if you just do things in the right order it makes everything so much easier. It takes the emotion and stress out of leading people, while keeping the vital connection, passion and empathy needed.

By understanding the central mindset and your own bias in relation to using Challenge and Support, and using all the tools available in the book, you will be able take stock of where you are and perhaps brush up one or two skills – the ones which will make a phenomenal difference to you right now. With these things in place you enable others to grow and shine in ways they never dreamed possible.

THE LIBERATOR

Helping others and being a part of their growth and development, making their lives easier and the world a better place is, I know, what many people aspire to. By following *The Liberator* process we believe you can do this. The approach described in the book will help you lead with strength, dignity and compassion.

The Liberator is the third in our series of three books. In our first book, *The Seeker*, we introduced a 6-Point Plan to guide you through things. The same 6-Point Plan appeared in the second book, *The Pioneer*. We introduce the same 6-Point Plan again here, to help your learning journey through The Mindset, Process and Skills of The Liberator.

6-Point Plan

1 / The Crux
2 / The Steps
3 / The Skills
4 / The Secrets
5 / The Gear Change
6 / The Impact

INTRODUCTION

We have a wonderful vision of you inspiring nations and generations to come.

We hope you enjoy it.

Best wishes
Ali

1
THE CRUX

PART 1: The Mirror
Background to the approach
Beyond mere management
The Leader-Developer approach
The new competencies for success
Implications for the Leader-Developer

PART 2: The Mindset
The Underlying Attitudes and Beliefs of effective Leader-Developers
The Mindset of High Challenge-High Support
Challenge and Support options: Choices and consequences
Organisation culture
Knowing your Challenge-Support profile
Rights and Responsibilities of Leader-Developers
Rights and Responsibilities of team members
Reinforcing concepts and attitudes
The OK Corral
Chapter summary

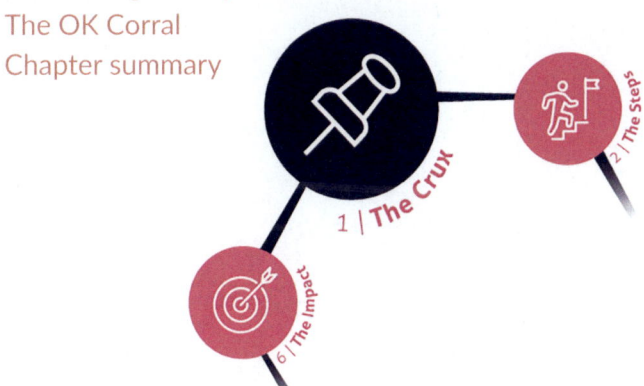

'Before you are a leader, success is all about growing yourself. When you become a leader, success is all about growing others.'
— Jack Welch

Part 1: The Mirror

Background to the approach

In his Foreword to the book, Paul Walkinshaw said: 'It champions tried and tested methods of leadership in organisations and it is a really good mirror for you to see yourself and change what you see to become the leader you aspire to be.'

By sharing the background of our approach, we hope it will give you the clarity you need to decide what kind of a leader you are and what footprint you would like to leave in the sand, and to make your style visible, consistent and authentic.

More help on developing your own personal style and legacy can be found in our earlier books in the series, *The Seeker* and *The Pioneer*, which set you up well for this stage. Here now, with our third book, *The Liberator*, we are giving you the blueprint for leading and developing high performance with ease and grace. It is akin to you holding up The Mirror so you can see yourself, how you align with the ethos and how you build an even more authentic approach as an inspiring leader of people.

The Liberator captures our research into what effective leaders, across a variety of industries, actually do when creating high performance. 'Creating' is not too strong a term here because, in the same set of circumstances, some leaders were highly effective, while many of their counterparts were much less so. It was as though some people had, in various ways, found an approach which really worked for them. And that approach was remarkably consistent across all the effective managers and range of industries, while the less successful managers operated to a much less cohesive or consistent approach.

What was sharply visible too, was that the more effective leaders were much more competent and comfortable in responding to the demands of today's organisational context, while the less effective ones, although perhaps having been successful in the past, were still struggling to come to grips with new ways of working.

We were encouraged, in the words of one of the people we worked with, to 'bottle' the best practice we found and thus make it available to others. Our experience since with thousands of leaders is that they strongly identify with the approach, and find the techniques and practices meaningful, practical and readily applicable.

Whether your need is to fine-tune your skills or cope well with a new set of circumstances, or whether you are becoming responsible for the performance of others for the first time, we hope, and sincerely believe, that sharing our approach with you will help.

Beyond mere management

The word 'management' is incredibly overused. It is the term most often used to describe those people responsible for the work and performance of others. Management literature is full of definitions of the term, typical among which is 'the process of planning, organising, directing and controlling the work of organisation members and of using all available organisational resources to reach stated organisational goals'.

Such descriptions do not come anywhere near to describing what those people responsible for the work and performance of others actually do when they are highly effective. Besides, much of the conventional theory and practices describe organisational life as it was, not as it is and will increasingly become. The times are not only 'a changing', to quote the song, they have changed and will continue to do so. In other words, the context of so-called management is radically different to what it was.

There is likely to be little argument that one of the imperatives in the millennium age is for high performance; organisations, and the individuals within them, are unlikely to survive the fierce competitive climate otherwise. High performance can be described in many ways, and certainly it is not just the effectiveness of doing the right things. This latter requires people at all levels to engage their judgement and use initiative responsibly.

One way of describing high performance in a team setting is the following set of results, which characterised all the high-performing teams we studied. But the first point to make is that…

…such results rarely happened by themselves, they were created; caused to happen by a leader who was not a mere manager.

As we will see, there was nothing magical about what such leaders did, and often what they did was largely intuitive or carried out at an 'unconscious competence' level. Their approach and the skills required are readily shared and trainable, which is what this book is about, and the results are easy to see.

The results of high-performance leadership

- Team all going in the same direction: Have a clear sense of purpose and can describe the same vision but in their own words.
- High morale and involvement: Feel positive about themselves, have Positive Regard for each other and the team leader, and have a strong sense of involvement and commitment to their work.

- High achievement: Purposeful, high levels of achievement, above average standards of performance in quality and quantity.

- Meet special demands: Deal with crises with vigour and resolution; see challenges and manage stress with fun and celebration.

- High reputation: Well known for the service they provide and the quality of their people; members tend to be promoted more and replacements are keen to join.

- Manage change: Embrace change; take change in their stride and cope effectively with new situations.

Clearly, this is not a sweat-shop situation, driven and compliant, but one with a momentum and impetus of its own. There is certainly high achievement, with very good output attained through the purposeful use of energy, where there is meaning to what is to be achieved through an owned sense of purpose. There is some fun, 'snap, crackle and pop' about it, so that special demands are met, not with weariness and moaning, but with zest, vigour and challenge. Members feel confident about themselves and their contribution (even in lower-level jobs), with high self-esteem, and also feel positive about other team members including the team leader, where there is mutual respect and understanding.

Such teams gain a reputation for themselves, and individuals become successful within them and, sometimes, move on to better jobs. The leader is generous enough to welcome and encourage this, knowing that they can grow replacements. Such teams, too, cope well with change for they have formed the habit of learning and of continuous improvement. Above all, such a way of working is a more natural, fulfilling and psychologically healthy place to be than is commonly the case in many work situations.

The frameworks that follow stem from research and observation of what effective leaders, across a variety of organisations and industries, actually do. There was a remarkable consistency in what such people believe, carry out and carry through. Because many of these highly effective people were working at the 'unconscious competence' level, it was only by observing how they went about the job that it was possible to see what differentiated them from less effective performers. It was then possible to set this in a framework of solid, underpinning theory and practice, so that the whole approach could be made congruent and readily accessible to others.

It was evident that some people had found the approach and skills almost randomly, while others, perhaps equally well intentioned, hadn't, and they were much less effective as a result. Yet the approach and skills required are available to, and can be acquired by, the vast majority of people who are responsible for the work of others, and this is our mission here.

The Leader-Developer approach

These highly effective people were Leader-Developers, which is the term we will use to describe them from now on.

'Leaders' in the sense that they did not just react to situations – they created the situation through their personal vision, energy and Transformational skills. They made a difference, not just being content to maintain smoothly the status quo.

'Developers' in the sense that part of their vision was to see their people performing at their very best, enabling and stimulating them to become the best they could be, and doing whatever was necessary to bring this about.

All this may sound charismatic and glamorous, requiring exceptional characteristics and skills. It isn't and it doesn't.

What it does require, however, is committing to an approach as a way of life, working to a themed process consistently and systematically, and anyone can learn it. It means developing The Mindset, The Process and The Skills of *The Liberator,* and being able to 'surf the waves of change' well, like this:

- **The Mindset:** These Leader-Developers have a key set of Underlying Attitudes and Beliefs, which they translate into practice through The Process and an associated set of Skills. More than anything else, the Underlying Attitudes and Beliefs matter. They provide the context, the rationale, the driving force for the whole, and The Mindset. So important are these Underlying Attitudes and Beliefs, that they will be explored in detail in Chapter 2. They are based not on the 'either/or' principle, but on the 'both/and' one of High Challenge and High Support, where both apply in powerful and equal combination.

- **The Process:** The Process gives a pathway, a systematic approach, and a track to run on. This is particularly useful and important for those new, or relatively new, to the task of leading and developing high performance. It provides a map or wiring diagram, as it were, where before there might only have existed uncertainty or confusion.

- **The Skills:** Many of The Skills which these highly effective Leader-Developers used are not generally given much emphasis in most management texts and training programmes. For example, Explicitness, getting to the root of issues, and the subtle use of rewards and consequences are rarely taught. Some of The Skills required are more commonly dealt with as stand-alone courses rather than a whole approach, such as Visioning, Questioning and Listening, and these we will spend less time on in order to concentrate on the crucial but less widely available ones. This will also allow more experienced managers to work from the base of what they already know.

- **Surf the waves of change:** Most importantly of all, the highly effective Leader-Developers we identified were much better equipped to deal with a changing environment and in enabling their people to respond well to it. The changing environment required not only working harder but working differently in a way that such effective Leader-Developers were already carrying out successfully. The Mindset required and the necessary Process and Skills to apply it are of crucial importance in responding to this ever-changing world in which we live. So, if competitive advantage is to come about through people, the way that competitive advantage is brought forth and used matters greatly.

The Leader-Developers and their way of working, provide the key to this.

The new competencies for success

In the organisation context just described, there are a number of paradoxes. While operating this way is arguably a more natural psychologically healthy way of working and being, as well as a more productive one, many such changes have not fulfilled what was expected of them, or have proved difficult to implement. One reason for this is that many managers felt ill-equipped to deal with this, concerned about what their job might be and whether they had the right level of skills to deal with it. This requires a different set of competencies to those which they have perhaps become used to. The requirement, simply stated, is to become a Leader-Developer.

Likewise, for many employees, a new context is experienced as more work, more hassle, more stress, with less fulfilment and reward. To understand why, for the moment, let us use an analogy...

> Many people have experienced change, often suddenly placed upon them, similar to being placed on top of a skyscraper without a parapet or railings, in the dark, and being asked to roller skate in intricate patterns. The response is to huddle in the safe territory of

> the middle of the roof, the risks being too great otherwise.
>
> If, on the other hand, the roof is well-lit, boundaries are defined (by way of railings in this instance) and skills are honed, then it is another matter indeed – the adventurous resourcefulness and skills displayed can be awesome.

While some have responded positively to the new opportunities, others have perhaps used their newly released initiative irresponsibly; the team leader is left with a confusingly wide range of responses to deal with, whereas before there was more comfortable and controllable uniformity.

The point is that to create a high-performing team in this new situation requires a different or additional set of competencies, founded on a particular mindset or paradigm. It is this which the highly effective Leader-Developers we worked with were operating to so successfully, and in a way which was significantly different from the average, or marginally performing, managers. As well as this our findings have been replicated by many other studies across all types of organisations, big and small – in manufacturing, sales, retail, financial services, local and central government, charities, health and education. What we have sought to do is to operationalise them and make them accessible, for they are readily learned, and will benefit anyone responsible for leading others to improve their own performance.

Implications for the Leader-Developer

Much of what we have to say can be seen as common sense, hopefully in a way whereby much of the fog which confuses the issues of leading and developing high performance can be dispersed. We take the view that if common-sense approaches to the ways in which people can better meet challenges, through being successful and thriving, becoming 'the best they can be', being more fulfilled and working better together, can be learned and applied, then this should be a cause for celebration, not scepticism.

The oddity for us is that the essentially authentic and common-sense approach that such effective Leader-Developers take is so unusual. There is no magic in their success and the people involved are not a newly discovered breed of superheroes. They are down-to-earth people who have learned the most effective ways of dealing with organisational issues, creating their own and their team's success.

The approach we have taken is to make accessible what such people actually do by linking together behavioural models, which reflect best practice, into an overall process. Our intent has been to do this in a way in which they can be both understood and applied, and which creates connections with people's own practical experience.

PART 1: THE MIRROR

The purpose of *The Liberator* is not to promote the latest 'theory', nor is it a prescription for a universal panacea. Rather it shares successful methods of enabling people to meet the needs of an ever-changing environment, with strength and dignity.

We believe the approach makes a, if not *the*, significant difference in creating success through people, which for many organisations is the most significant competitive advantage they have.

Part 2: The Mindset

The Underlying Attitudes and Beliefs of effective Leader-Developers

Successful Leader-Developers who achieve sustained high-performance share, above all, one thing in common. This emerged strongly from our research. What they had in common was their Underlying Attitudes and Beliefs. Such Leader-Developers do not walk around with a placard around their necks proclaiming what they believe in, rather they act them out, live them, breathe them, demonstrate them. When we discussed performance development with them it was clear that the beliefs were deeply held; it was as though they were permeated with them, just as a stick of rock carries its signature throughout its entire length. They were rock-like too in the way they held onto these beliefs, even when encountering difficulty and resistance, including those occasions when they were not entirely successful.

The way we see people and situations, the particular 'lens' we use, defines them for us and strongly influences the way we react and behave. Some people may see a glass half empty while others will see it half full. While one person may see another as worthwhile, competent

THE LIBERATOR

and with something to offer, another person's 'lens' will see that same person as 'not to be trusted', 'out to get me' or incapable and needing to be looked after.

Sometimes this 'lens' is called a paradigm. We prefer to call it Underlying Attitudes and Beliefs, or simply The Mindset. Whatever it is called, the way we respond to a situation, what we say and do, the action we take and the way we carry it out, will all flow from it. It is the 'mainspring' of the way we relate to and deal with people. Stephen Covey, in his book *The Seven Habits of Highly Effective People*, gives a great example of this.

> The scene is the New York subway early on a Sunday morning. All is quiet and peaceful as the train waits to depart; the passengers are reading their Sunday newspapers or enjoying a moment of quiet reflection. Then onto the train comes a man with some children. The children proceed to run up and down the corridors, pulling at newspapers and creating much noise and disturbance. The man (the father) just sits slumped in a seat, not interfering with what is going on.
>
> Eventually, Covey approaches the father intending to remonstrate with him to resolve the problem. (We can readily imagine Covey's feelings and the way he was seeing the situation at this stage.) After some discussion, the father says, 'I'm sorry, I've just come from the hospital, my wife has just died, I don't know how I am going to cope and my children don't either.'

Immediately, the same situation is seen through a different 'lens' or paradigm. Covey's immediate response to the news is to want to help, to support. Any punitive thoughts and bad feelings have fled, he is seeing the same situation differently through a new 'lens'.

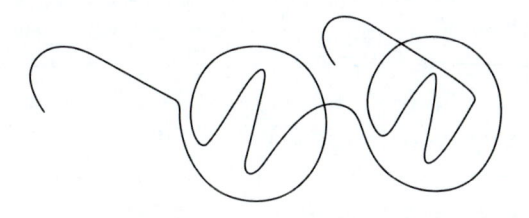

The most important characteristic for leading and developing high performance in others is The Mindset you have concerning your people. Without these Underlying Attitudes and Beliefs, you are unlikely to develop high performance in others. They underpin The Skills required, and without them, no matter how perfectly honed, The Skills are unlikely to be effective. In fact, the reverse is true; if you operate consistently with the right Underlying Attitudes and Beliefs you can achieve significant results, even though your Skills may not be completely perfect. Attitude is all.

> ### TOP TIP: ATTITUDE
> 'The longer I live, the more I realise the impact of attitude on life. Attitude, to me, is more important than facts. It is more important than the past, than education, than money, than circumstances, than

failures, than successes, than what other people think or say or do. It is more important than appearance, giftedness or skill. It will make or break a company... a church... a home.

'The remarkable thing is, we have a choice every day regarding the attitude we will embrace for that day. We cannot change our past... we cannot change the inevitable. The only thing we can do is play on the one string we have, and that is our attitude... I am convinced that life is 10% what happens to me and 90% how I react to it.

'And so it is with you... we are in charge of our attitude.'

— Charles R Swindoll

The Mindset of High Challenge-High Support

This set of Underlying Attitudes and Beliefs we call High Challenge-High Support. It is the deeply held and actioned frame of reference out of which Leader-Developers, who are mobilisers of human energy, act. Leading and developing high performance matters to these people; they do not simply go through the motions but instead invest themselves in The Process with passion, intensity and belief – hence the term High Challenge-High Support. Challenge in the sense that they have high standards and expectations about what can be achieved, Support in the sense that they care about their people's success and put themselves out to bring it about.

High Challenge-High Support is not 'either/or', it is 'both/and'. The concept challenges Leader-Developers to hold the two opposites in powerful and equal balance. Such Leader-Developers are, for example, prepared to push hard for increased quality of performance – even at the cost perhaps of losing some immediate popularity – and at the same time consistently give strong support and encouragement. They will deal with any emerging bad practices immediately, knowing that firm, early action will prevent a more developed situation from occurring which will cause more 'pain' to everyone to put right. They will trust people, but if anyone abuses that trust they will deal with them in no uncertain terms. They will both 'push' and 'pull' people through change, providing firmness of direction when necessary and the security of belief in people that they have the capability to win through. They will be direct and explicit in telling someone that a piece of work is not to the standard required and what is expected, and at the same time put themselves out to make sure the person succeeds. They are Developers, providing the impetus for people to stretch their boundaries and grow their capabilities, and the means through mentoring and coaching to do so. They are generous and tough enough to entrust people to use initiative, and at the same time to field genuine mistakes, treating such mistakes as an opportunity to learn and improve.

In previous years, the style of management could be broadly described as a 'push' one, but exercised in a command and control fashion; this was eventually seen as unproductive and having many negative consequences. So the conventional wisdom became to swing the pendulum in the opposite direction, to a 'pull' one, concentrating on encouragement, participation and counselling-based approaches.

In terms of McGregor's Theory X and Theory Y management styles, there has generally been a polarisation towards Y, but it seems both babies were thrown out with the bath water. However, McGregor was often misinterpreted; it is not the either/or of X and Y, but the both/and of Z, the ingredients of High Challenge-High Support. Another ingredient of High Challenge-High Support is the passion and intensity with which it is held. It is the both/and approach which so many Leader-Developers, when they come in contact with the concept, find so reassuring and 'grounding' as it fits with what they often intuitively feel is right.

> Theory X: People must be closely directed and controlled if they are to produce to standard.
>
> Theory Y: Participative management will of itself bring out people's natural abilities and motivation to do well.

PART 2: THE MINDSET

Support is a strong term. Roger Harrison gives a good description of Support when he talks about creating high levels of service in the workplace: 'this involves looking for, and acknowledging, the good and positive in people, listening to their hopes and fears, seeing them as valuable and unique, responding to their needs and nurturing their growth'.

But Support by itself can be lopsided or, as one chief executive put it when pointing out the risks both to the business and the long-term security of people if a 'soft', fool's paradise approach is taken:

> 'People, of course, are far and away the most important resource in any company. But they are more than that. It is very easy to forget when endeavouring to develop people and to care for them, and even to love them, that the needs of the business must come first. Without that, there can be no lasting security. A fool's paradise in which effort is concentrated only on the present well-being of the staff, without regard for the future, will eventually disintegrate and it may well be the staff that suffer most.'
> —K Barham, *Management for the Future*

An alternative way of looking at this point is:

> 'When the horses come to the forge it's the sentimental people who are the most trouble – so careful to be gentle that they forget to be firm;

31

the horses get confused; they don't know what they're supposed to do and they get nervous and restless, it's just as hurtful as being too rough.'
—**J Maxwell,** *The Blacksmith*

What we are talking about is both/and, that is both High Challenge and High Support used in powerful and equal combination.

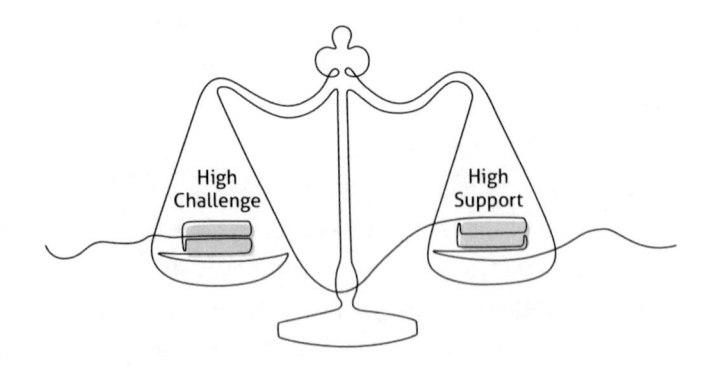

The same chief executive described this well:

> 'The needs of our business will be most effectively attained if the needs of people for fulfilment, success and meaning, are met. If people are in poor shape, the company's objectives are unlikely to be achieved. Yet the needs of the business still come first. People need to be developed, but this will not be achieved by treating them with 'soft care', by allowing issues to be smoothed over without being properly addressed. To treat people

without care will cause them, and therefore the business, to diminish.

'Experience suggests that the needs of people and the business will be best met if we treat ourselves with 'tough love' (ie care which does not shy away from tough decisions). This is very different from "macho" management which basically does not involve care. Tough love requires courage. Respect for the individual does not mean pandering to the individual's weaknesses or even wishes. Involving people through tough love to secure both their development and good performance requires managers to take the initiative.'
—**K Barham,** *Management for the Future*

We prefer the concept of High Challenge-High Support to 'tough love', as it describes more accurately what those high-performance leaders actually provide. Essentially, though, we are describing the same phenomenon, including the Leader-Developer causing things to happen – and taking the initiative.

Challenge and Support options: Choices and consequences

If the emphasis placed on both Challenge and Support varies from low to high, then there are four possible mindsets or positions a Leader-Developer can operate from at a given time:

THE LIBERATOR

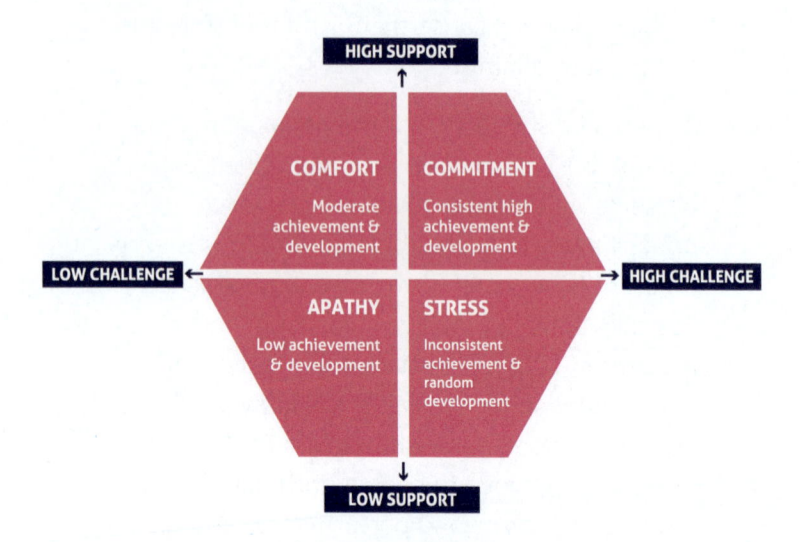

```
                    HIGH SUPPORT
                         ↑
              COMFORT  │  COMMITMENT
              Moderate │  Consistent high
           achievement │  achievement &
         & development │  development
LOW CHALLENGE ←────────┼────────→ HIGH CHALLENGE
              APATHY   │  STRESS
         Low achievement│ Inconsistent
           & development│ achievement &
                       │ random
                       │ development
                         ↓
                    LOW SUPPORT
```

Low Challenge-Low Support

This results in apathy, with low achievement and development. It is not a nice place to be; meaningless, nothing matters, no zest and fun, inward-looking and riddled with 'jobsworths', understandably so. Those people who join teams led this way come to realise that energy and enthusiasm are misplaced, no one takes any notice if you do good work, and there is little comeback if performance and quality are low. Why bother? Nothing seems to matter!

The manager who operates this way, perhaps out of a misguided view of participation or maybe because they feel a quiet life is what people want, is doing not only the organisation a disservice but, unfortunately, a major one to team members.

The first rule of warfare is said to be to defend your home base. That is, for most of us, the security of employment or employability. Team members who are managed in this way will lose their fitness to survive in today's world and will have an impoverished, unsatisfactory and poor-quality working life.

Low Challenge-High Support

This is the comfort position, where the expectations placed on people are moderate, but where they are well 'looked after' both materially and with courtesy, concern and attention. It is frequently an approach taken by paternalistic organisations (often benevolent ones) and at its heart is a dependency view of people. Here, The Mindset is that people want to, or should, remain Dependent on the greater expertise of others, typically their manager, rather than being more self-directing.

In this position moderate achievement and development are likely to occur. However, difficulties happen when change is encountered, either when there is a requirement for more to meet increasing standards from competition, or when new ways of doing things are required. Such organisations and teams often have the greatest difficulty in breaking out of comfort into doing new things, or doing the same things better, more so than even High Challenge-Low Support ones. Operating this way can indeed be to operate in a 'fool's paradise', as a hostage to fortune, with people not being 'the best they can be' but being complacently good enough for the present.

High Challenge-Low Support

This is the stress position, experienced by many organisational members in this rapidly changing era. It is stressful because although a few people thrive on High Challenge without Support, the majority of us do not, particularly in times of change when new boundaries have to be crossed. It is the 'sink or swim' version of leadership.

The problem with sinking or swimming is that some people don't ever learn to swim, and those who do often pick up faulty techniques. It is no wonder then that achievement is inconsistent, even though it can be moderate to high, and development is random because what is learned, if at all, is accidental. This is why, very often, attempts to make people 'empowered' have not altogether succeeded well. If Challenge is there without the Support enabling systems, such as reinforcement, encouragement and training, then such challenges are unlikely to be consistently and well met.

High Challenge-High Support

This is the place of commitment, where the Leader-Developer makes a difference by having both high expectations of what can be achieved, and actively enabling people to grow to meet such challenges. It is particularly important during change because successful change does not happen by itself – it is led, consolidated and sustained.

Such an approach equips team members to secure their own success, and to operate with Responsible Initiative and energy, rather than just being Dependent. It is not a 'big bang' approach but instead is founded on continuous improvement, step-by-step, led by the Leader-Developer until each team member takes on the approach themselves as a way of life.

This is the approach best guaranteed to generate a commitment to what needs to be achieved and to cause consistent high achievement and development. It was the one consistently applied by those Leader-Developers who led high-performance teams.

Organisation culture

Yet another perspective is given by looking at organisational culture – the way things are done around here – which will be the most suitable for your organisation, department or team. A useful framework for exploring culture proposed by Harrison (1972), describing four main types, and hybrids between them, is:

The Power Culture	Authoritarian and hierarchical, dominated by 'strong' leader(s), with an emphasis on status and politics.
The Role Culture	Also hierarchical, but with power exercised through rules, systems and procedures, with an emphasis on predictability and correctness. In its extreme form a bureaucracy.
The Achievement Culture	'Making a difference', actioning a purpose or goal to which the individual is committed, taking appropriate action to achieve useful things.
The Support Culture	Motivation and bonding through close, warm relationships, trust and care, co-operation, responsiveness and belonging.

The basic argument is that in today's fast-moving, competitive world cultures based on power or role are increasingly unsuitable for responsive organisations. They operate on an 'external' motivation or command and control principle. Instead, what is required is an achievement-based culture, and this, broadly speaking, is the direction many organisations are taking with their various change programmes under the labels of empowerment, TQM, customer service, organisational effectiveness or whatever.

While working in an achievement culture can provide opportunities for members to use their talents in ways which are more deeply satisfying, it can also make higher demands on its members' time and energy and, if unsupported, can lead to 'burnout'.

Also, changing a culture from, say, a role-based to an achievement-based one won't happen by itself, it needs support. However, as has been said, a support-based culture by itself, although bringing necessary ingredients such as co-operation, responsiveness, caring and commitment to others (which connect, among other things, to high customer service), has in-built weaknesses. For example, tough decisions about people may be postponed, or consensus overvalued, so that timely decisions are not made, or inadequate performance is not challenged. So, we are looking at a culture based on achievement and support – High Challenge-High Support, in fact.

The combination of the two, in powerful and equal balance, will also do much to alleviate the strain and stress that an achievement culture on its own can bring.

With High Challenge-High Support the motivation is 'internal', once the approach is established, rather than being externally driven and forced through, which brings about a different and more acceptable and sustainable relationship with the challenge of the job.

There is one further factor to take into account, and this is the notion of Personal Power. A power source is needed to cause achievement – nothing will happen without it – but it is a different kind of power than the one based on position and authority. Rather, it is based on the person and not the position; it is what we call Personal Power.

> **TOP TIP**
>
> Today success hinges on the ability to influence people to achieve common goals and purposes. This power to influence is personal effectiveness. It is the new power of competence. Such power is based on the *person*, not their *position*.
>
> It is... **Personal Power**.

Personal Power is the energy and influence source which fuels the Leader-Developer's effective use of the High Challenge-High Support approach. It is not the position held but what they do, what is believed, acted out and simply done. It is not the position but who is in the position which counts, their commitment and will to make a difference. Effective Leader-Developers define the situation for themselves, they are part of it, and if they use the 'lens' of High Challenge-High Support and demonstrate this consistently in practice, they will make that difference.

High performance in today's organisations requires increasingly the taking and acceptance of Responsible Initiative. This is one definition of that much-overused word 'Empowerment'.

Such enabled behaviour stems from power (empowerment) and underpins achievement. This is power based on the person, Personal Power again, and the development of such Personal Power in team members will be one of the goals of the effective Leader-Developer.

Knowing your Challenge-Support profile

The phrase High Challenge-High Support is used to describe and encapsulate the Underlying Attitudes and Beliefs which underpin *The Liberator* approach. These are the foundations on which the whole is firmly supported; without their enduring presence, any edifice of Skills will crumble and be experienced as just an edifice. You may not like the term High Challenge-High Support, but no matter, choose your own. What really matters is whether you adopt the principles and beliefs as a way of leading others and as the springboard for developing high performance with each and every one of your people.

At this stage, what is important is to review your current set of Underlying Attitudes and Beliefs in comparison with those Leader-Developers who have demonstrably secured consistently high performance. Reviewing your Underlying Attitudes and Beliefs in this way will enable you to reposition yourself, if necessary and if you choose to do so, and help to focus your own development.

It is likely that at present you will tend to incline either to the Support side or Challenge side; relatively few people, initially at least, are perfectly balanced in that they use both High Challenge and High Support powerfully and equally. In subsequent chapters, we will be dealing with The Steps and The Skills necessary to promote high performance, and you will be able to review your relative strengths and weaknesses in such Skills. Knowing whether you have a present tendency towards Support and therefore The Skills involved with this, or vice versa, will also help you with your own development plan.

Try the quick quiz that follows to identify your own Challenge-Support profile.

Underlying Attitudes and Beliefs: quick quiz

Look at the following points and circle a) or b) to indicate your preference:

1. All the people I work with:

    a) are basically OK people

    b) need to be stretched to find out what they are capable of

2. As the leader I have the responsibility to create:

    a) a clear vision and direction for the team

    b) a safe environment to build people's dignity and self-esteem

3. People must be treated with:

    a) courtesy and respect

    b) the firm belief and expectation that they can perform highly and successfully adapt to change

4. Communication must be:

    a) frank, genuine and not manipulative

    b) focused on everyone achieving the target

5. As the leader I have the right to:

    a) be direct in telling people what I expect from them and telling them when they are not delivering

    b) maintain momentum, output and harmony within the team

6. My overall aim is to:

    a) help everyone who works with me to be the best they can be and feel good about their contribution and competence

    b) achieve my vision of the team performing at its very best

7. In order to achieve my aim, I am prepared to:

    a) sacrifice immediate popularity to push people to realise their full abilities

    b) give them all the help and support I can to enable them to succeed

8. People who fundamentally disagree with my overall aim:

   a) have the right to do their own thing, elsewhere, and to go with my goodwill

   b) usually do their best if treated reasonably and fairly

Check your responses against the following guide to see whether they incline more towards Challenge or Support.

Inclined towards Support		Inclined towards Challenge	
1 a)		1 b)	
2 b)		2 a)	
3 a)		3 b)	
4 a)		4 b)	
5 b)		5 a)	
6 a)		6 b)	
7 b)		7 a)	
8 b)		8 a)	
Total		Total	

You will be able to make a judgement about the direction of your own views. Remember, though, that it is the combination of Challenge and Support (the both/and principle) that really matters.

Part of building your High Challenge-High Support profile is to set the ground rules clearly, by thinking about your Rights and Responsibilities as a Leader-Developer, and also those of the people who work with and for you.

Rights and Responsibilities of Leader-Developers

As a Leader-Developer, I have both Rights and Responsibilities. Equally, the people who work with and for me have Rights and corresponding Responsibilities.

My Responsibilities include:

- Creating a high-performance team, one which is capable of delivering what needs to be done tomorrow as well as today

- Providing a clear sense of direction to the people I lead

- Enabling people to achieve their full capability, even though this might not be immediately popular

- Being genuine, saying what I mean and meaning what I say and treating others with respect and frankness

- Giving of myself and my support, to enable the people in my team to succeed and being delighted when they do

- Letting people know how they are performing, continually, through strong, clear feedback
- Causing people to stay 'fit', for their sake as well as mine, in today's competitive world

My Rights include:

- Demanding the same level of courtesy and frankness that I give
- Telling people what is expected of them, clearly and explicitly
- Letting them know when they are not performing through direct unambiguous feedback
- Setting the vision for the team and driving for its attainment.

This means adopting and living by the principle of

HIGH CHALLENGE – HIGH SUPPORT

Rights and Responsibilities of team members

Equally, team members have Rights, which include:

- Being treated with courtesy and respect
- For there to be a clear sense of direction – including knowing what is expected of them and the standard required
- Not following my vision, if they cannot agree with it – but following their own vision elsewhere
- Being regarded as a fundamentally OK person – who has the inherent ability to succeed and perform highly
- Knowing how they are getting on – regularly

With the rights go Responsibilities, including:

- Respecting the rights of the Leader-Developer
- Treating the Leader-Developer with courtesy and respect, equal to that given
- Performing highly and meeting the standards expected of them
- Continuously striving to learn, to grow and to improve their capability
- Doing all they can to enable the team, as a whole, to succeed

Reinforcing concepts and attitudes

As well as holding firmly to and practising the Underlying Attitudes and Beliefs of High Challenge-High Support, the effective Leader-Developers of high performance we worked with also operated according to two crucial concepts which pervaded what they did. There were, in addition, two attitudinal characteristics which were important to them. Although they did not see them as an established theoretical underpinning for what they did, they are, in fact, just that.

The CONCEPTS	Expectations Theory Reinforcement Theory
The ATTITUDES	Positive Regard Genuineness

Expectations Theory

Expectations Theory is basically very simple. If expectations are high, you tend to get more. If expectations are low, you tend to get low or moderate performance. Effective Leader-Developers of high performance always have high expectations about their people's performance and ability to develop and change, and work on this basis. It is a classic case of 'you get what you give'.

Having low expectations of someone is like putting a curse on the person; it inhibits them from getting in touch with their real abilities, confidence and competence. It often confirms their own low self-esteem or view of the world. It reinforces, negatively. It is disempowering. Leader-Developers who operate from High Support without corresponding High Challenge, often cause others to remain Dependent on them rather than causing them to grow their own competence and capability.

The reverse is equally true. This is not to say that everyone is capable of becoming a brain surgeon. We are not talking about driving people beyond their capabilities but, equally, their potential capabilities are likely to be larger than they, and possibly you, presently think. Small victories and successes themselves change people's own expectations, raising the possibility and expectations of further successes, that success is possible and is the norm. This reinforces positive self-esteem which, in turn, leads to more growth and success.

The effective Leader-Developers of high performance we encountered all had high expectations about what their people were capable of – and it mattered and it showed.

Expectations, high or low, are rather like body language in that it leaks and people will pick up the signals and know how to respond. Also, your expectations will affect the way you approach, deal with and interact with people, generating an effect of its own.

Many scientific experiments have confirmed this with remarkable consistency.

> Instructors at a welding school were told that the brightest group of trainees were the least able, and vice versa. The group which was the less able but who the instructors believed were the most able achieved the best results.

What seems to be the case, as a general rule, is:

- You get what you give
- If you're prepared to be disappointed then you won't be disappointed

The effective Leader-Developers were not naïve about this, but they held it as an important principle. They also had the sense to see that to get to the end result they had in mind they had to proceed in stages, by working to a process of continuous improvement. The complementary theory to expectations is 'expectancy', and basically this says that people will come to a decision as to whether the outcome required is worth the effort they would need to put in or the reward they would get; or whether the difficulty and effort was too great and the reward too low for the value of the outcome as they saw it. In starting the process of developing high performance, based on high expectations, 'chunking' the whole into more digestible stages, is likely to be most successful, particularly if each step achieved is reinforced. It can also, very often, develop a momentum of its own.

There is, too, one other important aspect of high expectations. This concerns the context of the workplace, simple but important standards like timekeeping, safety, the working environment, etc. To put it crudely, if your expectations about these are low, or allowed to slip, then it is unrealistic to expect people to buy into the notion of high performance. For these things are exemplars and poor standards with such basic functions will diminish what you are trying to achieve with everyone performing at their very best. It is similar to the so-called 'broken window' phenomenon, where it is known that if a broken window is not attended to then there is a much greater risk of the building being vandalised than in the case where the window is repaired immediately and standards maintained. So it is with your expectations of high performance; the broken window theory holds good here.

Reinforcement Theory

Effective Leader-Developers also had a strong intuitive feel for the reinforcement principle. In practice, this means 'catching people doing something right', instead of only paying attention when things go wrong. They operated this way, again as a way of life, not just once a year at a formal appraisal review, but hour by hour, day by day, week by week. They looked out for improvements and reinforced them with strong positive feedback, encouraging people to do more of the same, as a way of continuously developing competence in small but important steps. At the same time, they were prepared to, and gave, negative feedback when necessary as part of the whole. In both cases they used a subtle blend of rewards, and penalties or consequences, largely coming from themselves.

This is no mere Pavlovian 'stimulus-response' type conditioning. True, in the earlier stages of the process, stimuli of various kinds may be needed to get the response of a particular behaviour, and that behaviour may need to be reinforced. But the aim of these effective Leader-Developers was to get the person to learn, releasing the person's own creativity, in a way where the learning becomes a self-motivated activity. When this happens, the motivation source becomes not the 'push' one of externally applied rewards or punishments, but the 'pull' ones which come from the 'internal' motivation of the person themselves.

Again this comes back to the attitude of the Leader-Developer as well as their skills. For one thing, effective ones are prepared to invest the effort and persistence. They see their people not as an accident about to happen, but as a great achievement about to unfold. One team member expressed it all succinctly when commenting on his team leader:

> 'He spoke to me as an equal, kicked my ass when I'd done something wrong, praised me when I did something right. He was very good at communicating what was wanted and in keeping me involved. I thought I was important and I responded. I knew what was expected of me and I felt part of a team. It was down to me and I felt guilty if I didn't get the result.'

Positive Regard and Genuineness

Highly effective Leader-Developers of high-performance share two characteristics in common with effective counsellors. Research shows that effective counsellors need to have these two characteristics before they can help their clients and, if they don't display these characteristics, then their clients won't respond to them. These findings are extremely relevant to the way in which you discuss with someone their job performance and help them to improve.

The two attitudinal characteristics are:

Positive Regard	Genuineness
This means having respect for the other person as an individual and a positive belief in them as a person. Irrespective of the behaviour they are displaying, you see the good in them and view them as a decent human being.	This means that you are able to express your own feelings and tell the truth about your reaction to another person's behaviour. It means being direct, open and honest with the other person, not shying away from difficult conversations.

Without these underlying characteristics, you are unlikely to cause the other person to change and enhance their performance. Also, without them, the interaction is likely to be experienced as false, patronising or manipulative. With them, however, not only is the process destined to go well, but the interaction does not have to be technically perfect in order to be successful.

In other words:

- The underlying attitudes of Positive Regard and Genuineness, which underpin High Challenge-High Support, are even more important than the skills of conducting the discussion.

- Without them you will have little real influence on other people, particularly those whose performance you wish to help to improve significantly.

PART 2: THE MINDSET

It is better to engage with the other person directly, as a human being, and not hide behind the façade of being always measured and dispassionate. It is about being straight with the other person while valuing them as an individual.

Clearly, this does not mean losing your temper or over-reacting. Rather, it is concerned with having sufficient Positive Regard for the other person to 'tell it like it is', concentrating on what they do (the behaviour) that is causing good or poor performance. It is the part of Positive Regard which values the person, but not necessarily their behaviour.

If you keep your feelings bottled up, they will leak out anyway through body language and may be misinterpreted. Alternatively, they will come out at a later stage with irritation or anger. Also, if the interaction is not open and honest, or worse still is manipulative, then the other person will soon sense this. You can rarely keep feelings as hidden as you think you can.

Genuineness is part of Positive Regard and it is not possible to maintain Positive Regard without being Genuine. Both are essential for *The Liberator*, and to achieve a perfect balance of High Challenge and High Support.

Another useful perspective is the OK Corral, which we'll look at next.

The OK Corral

The OK Corral is derived from Transactional Analysis, which is a method of looking at relationships between people. It describes a fundamental way of being which affects the way we see and respond to others.

From an early age, people develop a view of their own worth and tend to take 'life positions' relative to other people. Life positions develop from experiences, particularly those during childhood, and affect the way people feel, act and relate.

The OK Corral Model is concerned with two basic views which you will operate to, perhaps subconsciously, when dealing with another person.

Firstly, how you view yourself:

- **I'm OK:** My self-esteem is reasonably high, I feel comfortable with this environment, I feel able to cope.

- **I'm not OK:** I'm uncomfortable dealing with this sort of issue, I don't feel I have the necessary skills, and I feel unable to cope.

Secondly, how you view the other person:

- **You're OK:** You have a right to your opinions, you are essentially decent, you have a contribution to make.

PART 2: THE MINDSET

- **You're not OK:** You never listen, you are wrong, you won't win this one.

The combination of your view of yourself and your view of the other person gives the possibility of four positions or attitudes. Each position is typified by particular types of behaviour.

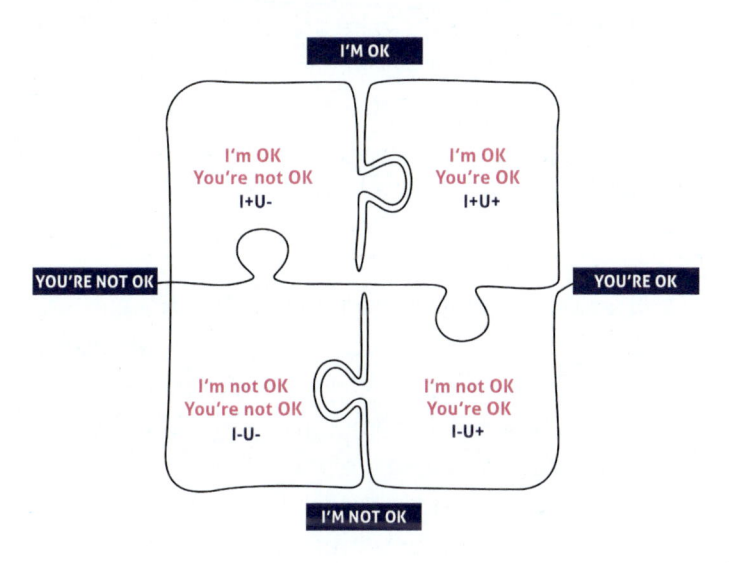

```
                    I'M OK

        I'm OK              I'm OK
     You're not OK         You're OK
        I+U–                 I+U+

YOU'RE NOT OK                           YOU'RE OK

      I'm not OK            I'm not OK
     You're not OK          You're OK
        I–U–                  I–U+

                   I'M NOT OK
```

Descriptions of OK Corral quadrants

- **I+U–**
  If this is your underlying attitude then your behaviour will indicate a feeling of superiority, either through an aggressive stance or alternatively an over-protective approach. This is likely to provoke resistance, aggressiveness or Dependence from the other party. It is either a High

57

Challenge-Low Support or Low Challenge-High Support one.

- **I−U−**

    This attitude manifests itself in a suspicious and often hostile approach to others, with an underlying feeling of 'Why bother, it won't make any difference anyway'. To be on the receiving end of this type of behaviour can be frustrating and exhausting, and it requires considerable effort to deal with it appropriately. It comes in the Low Challenge-Low Support category.

- **I−U+**

    If you're viewing life from this position on the OK Corral, it is likely that your self-esteem has taken a knock; you are strongly influenced by the other person, who is OK in your mind. Your behaviours emanating from here are dependent, nonassertive and often yielding, which in turn can lead to a further dip in your self-esteem. It is another Low Challenge-High Support position. An interesting factor about those who often inhabit this quadrant is the lightning switch they can make to I+U−, and when the final straw is delivered, the method of dealing with it is often an extremely aggressive approach which surprises all parties.

- **I+U+**

    This is the most productive position to occupy, whenever possible. Behaviours are assertive but warm, and the underlying attitude is one of Positive Regard and trust, even when delivering bad news or a potentially unpleasant message. Your expectations of the other person are consistently high; when expectations are high, and supported by Positive Regard and Genuine behaviour, the chances of those expectations being met are significantly increased. This is the High Challenge-High Support position.

Effective Leader-Developers operate from the I+U+ position, consistently, even at times of difficulty, and when dealing with poor performers whose position in the OK Corral is I-U+, I+U- or, most difficult of all, I-U-. There are a number of powerful reasons for this:

- Being on the receiving end of I+U- behaviour promotes Dependency or Counter-Dependency and rebellion

- Being on the receiving end of I-U- behaviour promotes withdrawal and alienation

- Being on the receiving end of I-U+ behaviour promotes Dependency and acquiescence

- Being on the receiving end of I+U+ behaviour promotes Independence and Interdependence

Therefore, in any situation where you are about to have a performance development conversation with someone, stop, breathe, wait... check what thoughts

THE LIBERATOR

are going on in your head. You want to ensure the best possible outcome.

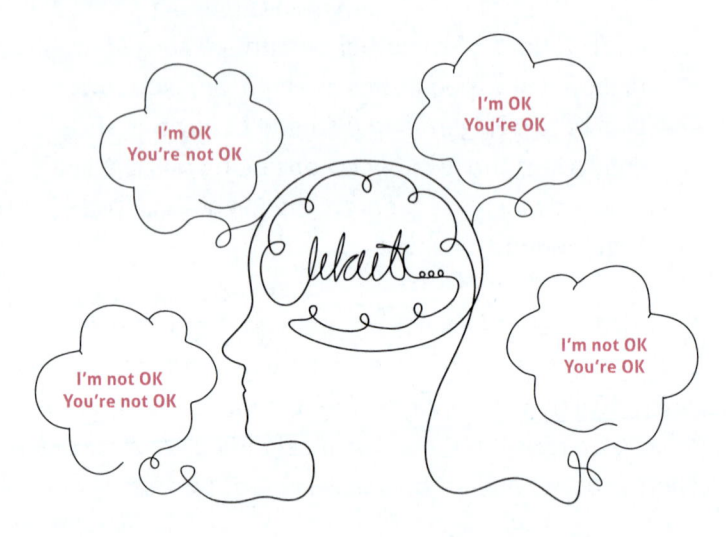

I'm OK / You're not OK

I'm OK / You're OK

wait...

I'm not OK / You're not OK

I'm not OK / You're OK

Enabling someone to be the best they can be and performing at their best means them not acting Dependently or rebelling against you and the organisation with Counter-Dependence, but having the attitudes, abilities, skills, confidence and competence to manage tasks Independently and, better still, Interdependently.

This is the mission of the Leader-Developer.

Chapter summary

Part 1: The Mirror

The Liberator:

- Lives by the approach described here, which is based on practical research into what effective leaders actually do to bring about sustained high performance.

- Is a Leader-Developer, not just a manager; what they do causes high performance to happen. They look in The Mirror and this is what they see.

- Knows this is not a sweat-shop activity, but rather an approach founded on a mindset, a Process and a set of Skills or competencies, which benefit all the stakeholders.

- Demonstrates an approach which is readily available and can be learned by all; it does not need charismatic heroes to fulfil it. What it does require is a set of competencies which are presently not widely taught.

- Has high-performance competencies, which are particularly important in the organisational context of today, where change has a major impact on the way of working. These competencies equip Leader-Developers to cope well with inevitable further change.

Part 2: The Mindset

The Liberator:

- Holds a strong set of Underlying Attitudes and Beliefs which they work to, consistently and in a way which is clearly visible to others.

- Operates to the principle of High Challenge-High Support, used in powerful and equal combinations. It is not either/or but both/and.

- Understands the context and culture they are working in and uses their own Personal Power to promote necessary change through a High Challenge-High Support approach, developing not only their team members' skills and abilities but also their own Personal Power.

- Knows their own bias to Challenge and Support, takes this into account, and seeks to develop their approach so that they are both used, consistently, in powerful and equal balance.

- Has a clear view of their Rights and Responsibilities as the Leader-Developer, and also the Rights and Responsibilities of those who work with them.

- Operates with high expectations of their people and what they can achieve. At the same time, they work toward a cumulative series of attainable goals, taking a step-by-step approach, while keeping their overall goal of enabling the team and its members to become the best they can be.

- Has Positive Regard for others, which means having respect for them as an individual and a positive belief in them as a person. Equally, they are Genuine, in being direct, open and honest with the other person.

- Feels that they are OK and so is the other person (I+U+) and keeps on feeling this way even in times of difficulty – when they are able to see that it is not the other person who is not OK, but the person's behaviour.

- Does not want their people to remain or become Dependent on them, but sees their role to enable people to develop not only their skills and knowledge but also their confidence, willpower and ability to manage tasks Independently and Interdependently.

2

THE STEPS: WHAT HIGH-PERFORMING LEADER-DEVELOPERS ACTUALLY DO

The 4-Step Process: Visioning, Mobilising, Developing, Enabling
The 4-Step Process
The Mindset, The Steps and The Skills Combined
Leadership or management – what's the difference?
The 4-Step Process explored
Summing up The 4-Step Process and 15 Skills
Chapter summary

'The best executive is one who has sense enough to pick good men to do what he wants done, and self-restraint to keep from meddling with them while they do it.'
— Theodore Roosevelt

The 4-Step Process: Visioning, Mobilising, Developing, Enabling

The 4-Step Process

What effective Leader-Developers actually do when maximising performance and people's potential is to follow a simple four-step process. They work at The Process constantly and with resolution. A number of skills are involved but, no matter how good their skills are, their application will not be truly effective unless used as part of a consistent process and with the right mindset. The Process gives those leading others, and those new to such experience in particular, a 'track to run on' and a direction along which they can proceed with a sense of reassurance.

And this is The 4-Step Process. You start at the bottom and work up.

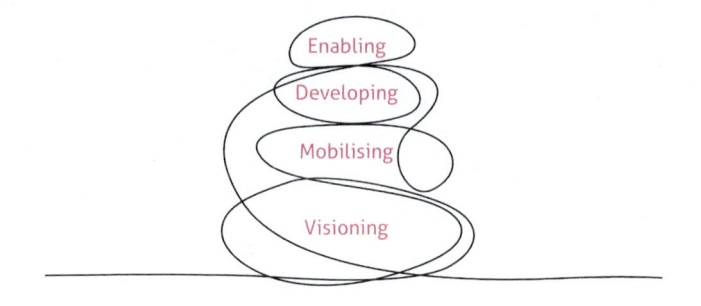

Enabling
Developing
Mobilising
Visioning

What is noticeable about Leader-Developers is that they rigorously apply The 4-Step Process with every member of their team. It is a fluid and continuous process, where the Leader-Developer selects the most appropriate step for the situation, with grace, dignity and compassion. They know that flexing their style appropriately, and even going beyond their own comfort zone, will give their people the best chance of success. They liberate their people and allow them to shine.

The Mindset, The Steps and The Skills Combined

When identifying what high-performing Leader-Developers actually do, it became clear there was a set of fifteen distinct Skills which flow through The 4-Step Process. These Skills, when combined with The Mindset of High Challenge-High Support, within the structure of The 4-Step Process, made the combined whole even more empowering for all.

They all come together like this:

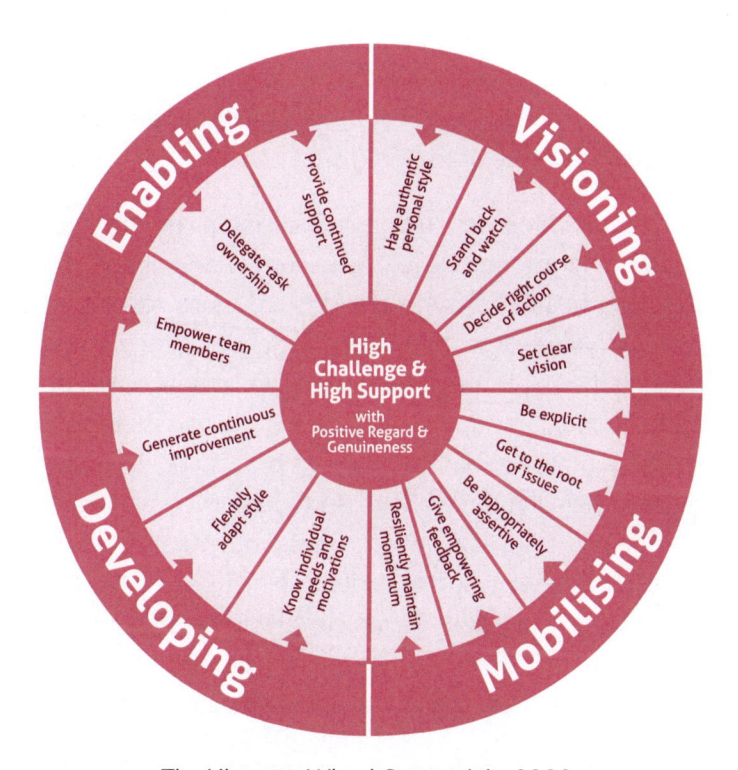

THE 4-STEP PROCESS: VISIONING, MOBILISING, DEVELOPING, ENABLING

*The Liberator Wheel © copyright 2023,
Ali Stewart & Co and Dr Derek Biddle*

The Skills are presented in more detail, as a full set of competencies, at the end of this chapter.

Leadership or management – what's the difference?

Before exploring The 4-Step Process, it's useful to clarify the difference between leadership and management as it greatly affects the way the whole process is used and applied.

You will have noticed that we use 'leaders' rather than 'managers' when describing the developers of high performance. Those effective Leader-Developers of high performance we encountered most certainly held a leadership view of their roles.

One of the differences between leadership and management is that Leader-Developers identify and action the direction to take, while managers are more concerned with carrying things out in good order. Imagine a group hacking its way through the jungle. The manager will be there, working hard, making sure that the machetes are sharp, wiping sweat from fevered brows, looking after the well-being of the workers, and keeping morale high – all essential tasks. The leader, on the other hand, will, in addition, be the person who climbs up a tree to scout the way ahead. The leader is concerned with a future direction, not with just maintaining well the status quo. So it is when you are leading and developing high performance.

Another way of defining the difference is that 'managers do things right, Leader-Developers do right things'. Leader-Developers make a difference and add value. Change needs leadership; it doesn't happen by itself, at least not well, and much development is concerned with change, and change with development. Leader-Developers are part of the situation and define it.

THE 4-STEP PROCESS: VISIONING, MOBILISING, DEVELOPING, ENABLING

There are three levels of leadership:

- **Non-Leadership:** Leaders avoid decisions, withdraw when needed, are uninvolved and take no stand.

- **Transactional Leadership:** Leader-Developers determine what their people need to do to achieve objectives, clarify those requirements, then help and ensure they are achieved.

- **Transformational Leadership:** Leader-Developers, through their personal vision and energy, inspire their people and have a major input. Such leaders motivate people to achieve and develop much more than would be thought possible, and help connect them with the energy of their own internal motivation and needs.

Transactional Leaders tend to be primarily action orientated, whereas Transformational Leaders tend to have, and use, a higher degree of vision. Vision has to do with creating images of future goals while action has to do with the execution of immediate behaviours. Both are necessary and define *The Liberator* approach. The Transactional approach is needed in the earlier stages of The Process particularly, while the Transformational approach gets people to realise their true potential and become the best they can be. It's a case of not either/or but both/and.

> 'Vision without action is just a dream.
> Action without vision just passes the time.
> Vision with action can change the world.'
> — Joel A Barker

THE LIBERATOR

Not everyone is a charismatic Napoleon, Wellington, Churchill or Ghandi – thank goodness. We are not talking about charisma here, but a set of Skills, underpinned by The Mindset of High Challenge-High Support, applied within The Process and carried out with Personal Power, rather than positional power.

It's now time to explore The Process and The Skills in more detail.

Assume you have been asked to take on a new group or department, so you will be looking at a situation afresh.

The 4-Step Process explored

Step One: Visioning

> V1: Have an authentic personal style: Project and consistently hold a clear personal style and a strong sense of who you are and what you stand for, which is clearly visible to others.

Often the most challenging job is a person's first leadership one, no matter how junior in the organisation. This is particularly so if you are assuming leadership of a group of which you are already a member. The

THE 4-STEP PROCESS: VISIONING, MOBILISING, DEVELOPING, ENABLING

immediate issue is how you should relate to people in the group. This also applies, albeit to a lesser extent, to more experienced Leader-Developers.

At the one extreme there are those leaders who position themselves to be aloof, hostile even, while at the other, some leaders try to form buddy-buddy relationships with their team members. There are dangers involved in both these extremes – being approachable and friendly without either trying to be 'one of the lads', or being aloof, is usually the best choice to make. This enables you to both stay in contact with people and, at the same time, deal with any inappropriate behaviour, without being seen as two-faced. Being Genuine and

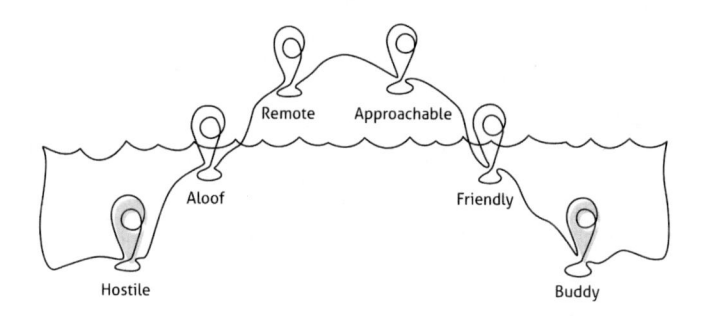

Remote — Approachable
Aloof — Friendly
Hostile — Buddy

having Positive Regard for team members, is an integral part of this.

One of the fears that Leader-Developers who are new to a group are often concerned with is how they will be regarded by the group. 'Will I be liked by them?',

THE LIBERATOR

'Will I be respected?', 'Will they set out to give me a hard time?' What is important in the situation is to have a clear set of personal standards, to live by them and make them visible to others. In almost all groups where a new leader is introduced, there is some testing out of the new leader to establish what the ground rules are, and test the boundaries.

It may involve only one person but the rest of the group will be watching. If the new leader does not deal with the situation in a way which is consistent with what they stand for then, at minimum, a lot of ground will be lost.

In this initial stage, you are unlikely to have yet a distilled view about the future direction and what can be improved. If, however, you hold and project a clear personal style and a strong sense of what you stand for, which is clearly visible to team members, then this is helpful to them. From the perspective of the team, if the new team leader is enigmatic or guarded, this can add to the stress and uncertainty in what already may be a difficult situation for them. On the other hand, if it is clear what the leader stands for and what is important to them – the 'rules of engagement' so to speak – people know where they are. It helps enormously if what you stand for is firmly rooted in the beliefs of High Challenge-High Support.

What also matters is that such an approach is consistently carried out. It should not depend on what side of the bed you got out of that morning, or how you

THE 4-STEP PROCESS: VISIONING, MOBILISING, DEVELOPING, ENABLING

feel at the moment, or whether you personally like or dislike the person you are dealing with. This is so people will catch on quickly that behaving in one way will get a response from you, and behaving in another way will produce a different response. You will be seen as authentic, which is reassuring for your team.

V2: Stand back and watch: Listen and question effectively to establish facts and information; consult with others to get views; perceptively observe differences between what is said and done, and where improvements can be made.

Leader-Developers make a difference and add value. So the first stage in the process is to see where improvements in performance can be made. This means reviewing present directions and levels of performance thoroughly and well, being careful to identify the 'good' as well as the 'less good', and not throwing the baby out with the bathwater.

This can be achieved by gathering data and information obtained from observation, and by good quality questioning and listening to others.

At this stage, there are some traps to avoid:

- One trap is moving forward blindly, perhaps based on assumptions, without a proper diagnosis

75

of the situation. This is sometimes brought about by the self-image of the tough action person, who knows right from wrong, and who gets things 'sorted' right away.

- Another is the 'hero' syndrome, where the expectation is (either self-imposed or imposed by the 'hero' boss) that miracles will be wrought in the first few days, if not hours.

- And then there are those who have the solution (usually ready-made) before understanding the problem. They leave a trail of ravaged, damaged groups, departments and even companies in their wake.

So, a key skill of Leader-Developers is taking time to step back and watch and consult with others, observing differences between what is being said and done, and taking time to gather data and information, to ensure these traps are avoided.

> V3: Decide the right course of action: Analyse the present situation accurately by seeing above the waves; sift information and form views without jumping to conclusions; manage complexity without becoming submerged by it and decide the right course of action.

THE 4-STEP PROCESS: VISIONING, MOBILISING, DEVELOPING, ENABLING

It is time now to analyse the situation accurately; it is the leader who will need to sift the information, come to conclusions and set out the path.

It may be that performance in the team is uniformly high already, or it may be that it is a lot less than that. Whatever the situation, there is always a case for enhancing performance still further. In the case of already high performers, as the saying goes, 'You don't have to be ill to get better.'

Taking time to 'see above the waves', sifting through all the information gathered while keeping an open mind, then analysing what needs to be done and deciding the right course, is crucial during this Visioning Step.

Whatever the situation now, once the analysis is done, it's necessary to start visualising future possibilities, not just managing and monitoring the status quo of the present. Deciding the right course of action allows you then to create a compelling vision.

> **V4: Set a clear vision:** Create your vision with a clear sense of direction, transmit your enthusiasm for and commitment to it; envision everyone in the team performing at their *very* best and being the best they can be.

A vision is the image we have of a desired future state. It is like stepping forward in time and seeing things as they will be. The vision gives a future direction, which can be made to happen, rather than simply reacting to events. It gives meaning and purpose to what we do.

Images are powerful and sometimes scary things. They set out the challenge we place on ourselves if we are to convert them to concrete reality. They also focus our energies on doing 'the right things' and can sustain our direction and persistence when things sometimes don't go smoothly and our resilience is gnawed at.

What effective Leader-Developers have in common is a strong, clear vision, generated by them, and to which they are committed. This vision includes the task, business or technical developments and it is also strongly concerned with people. They envision the team and every member within it performing at their best, being the best they can be, and using their full potential. For they know that, when it comes to achieving full effectiveness, it is people who make the difference.

As one chief executive put it:

> 'Long term we have no sustainable competitive advantage in capital investment, technology or scale. Our real potential competitive differentiation is our people and how effectively they contribute to the business.'

THE 4-STEP PROCESS: VISIONING, MOBILISING, DEVELOPING, ENABLING

Having a view of people performing at their best is not just a Transactional one, but a Transformational one. People's capability and capacity are enlarged in a way that they become self-actualising and internally motivated, working towards Independence and Interdependence rather than just through command and control. This is the meta vision Transformational Leader-Developers hold on to: belief in and taking action through their High Challenge-High Support approach. So, it is more than skills and knowledge that such Leader-Developers grow in others. It is attitudes, self-belief, confidence and self-direction. They are true 'empowerers'.

All this may sometimes seem difficult, if not impossible, to achieve, perhaps particularly so when compared with the reality of present performance levels. Visioning is also something that not everyone finds easy.

One way to do it is to follow these steps:

- Let your mind project forward, say, one or two years into the future.
- Write down your vision for how your team will be performing at its very best. Describe in concrete terms what they will actually be doing and how you will know they are succeeding. You don't need an essay, just a few statements.
- Now do this for the individual members of the team. Hang on to your belief that you can make a

difference, even though you may currently have some poor or limited performers.

- The next step is to stay where you are in the future and look back to the present situation, visualising the journey between the two situations as a flight of steps. Imagine each team member climbing the steps to join you, at different speeds perhaps, and starting from different positions, but coming to join you. You will know the step each person is starting from by virtue of the analysis of the current situation you have carried out, having identified the key ones and priority areas.

Achieving the vision means working in a series of small steps. It's like eating an elephant – it can only be done one mouthful at a time. Nothing will change, certainly not in any focused, concerted way unless you cause and enable it to do so.

If you don't have a vision, and thus a direction, any movement will be accidental, and you could end up in the 'wrong' place, or just drift.

This brings us back to Vision and Action again. 'Vision without action is just a dream; action without vision is meaningless and boring; vision with action can change the world'. The action is in the purposeful doing, which we will explore further when looking at the Mobilising Step of The Process.

THE 4-STEP PROCESS: VISIONING, MOBILISING, DEVELOPING, ENABLING

It may be that your team are high performers already; highly skilled, capable and motivated. But this does not mean that they can stand still and, anyway, it is unlikely that they will all be 'perfect' or have achieved professional mastery. The same principles apply; the difference is that your task is an easier one, but equally one with more responsibility, for taking the soft option of pretending everything is perfect, or allowing the team to stand still or slip, is to do them an injustice. The level of ability, experience and commitment in the team may also be such that you will want to involve them more fully in the vision building, but it is the Leader-Developer who will need to make the final judgements as they are best positioned to do so.

You have a direction, a vision, which includes a picture in your mind's eye of each and every member of your team performing to their full potential. You may be seeing ordinary people doing extraordinary things which they don't yet know they are capable of doing. You may be seeing a winning team operating in a new way, thriving on change, and reaching new levels of competence. You may be envisioning habitually Dependent people, reluctant to change their ways, who become empowered, decisive and highly productive. You may be envisioning already successful people achieving improved results with less stress and more enjoyment.

None of this is likely to happen by itself. It is the leader who can make the difference – not overnight usually, but steadily, step-by-step, by consistently and patiently working to a process which involves key steps and priority areas. It is the Leader-Developer who will make the crucial influence.

It is time too, to share that vision, that future perspective, with your team. You know where you and your group are going and it's time to start the journey. Knowing where you are going, keeping the goal firmly in mind, and being clear about what you want to achieve with and for your team, will enable you to maintain direction, as well as meet and overcome the difficulties which will inevitably occur.

Step Two: Mobilising

The Mobilising Step comes before the Developing one. 'Developing' means increasing participation. There is example after example, however, of groups with new leaders, or those reformed or reorganised through change, not altering the way they operate and having diffuse and varying goals. To move straight into high participation as a basis for development, without having first established and reinforced the direction and the standards required, is to promote misunderstanding and future difficulty.

Like 'motherhood and apple pie', participation is regarded as a 'good thing' – it is – but in terms of its

THE 4-STEP PROCESS: VISIONING, MOBILISING, DEVELOPING, ENABLING

effectiveness the ground has to be prepared first. We are not talking about heavy-handed or repressive 'leadership' here or a return to the old command and control methods. On the contrary, it's light but firm, and enabling. It's an approach which has high expectations of people's capability to contribute excellently, coupled with High Support to enable them to achieve that contribution.

The problem can be that the team may have become complacent, or individual members have done it 'this way' for the last 700 years. Or they may be comfortable in the security of the known, or they are not ambitious about their own performance capability. To disturb the status quo may often not be popular at first, or generate resistance, and this is where holding on to the principles of High Challenge-High Support becomes particularly important. Sometimes a new leader will find that the group is already functioning well, with a clear and uniform sense of direction which only needs fine-tuning, and operating to a level of ability and commitment which is exceedingly high. In such cases, the leader's task could be easy, or it could be more difficult – for if a change in direction is required, it will be like turning the proverbial oil tanker.

The Mobilising Step is about establishing the future direction, standards required, and the way of operating and aligning and connecting people to the vision,

THE LIBERATOR

so they become committed to it. It may involve breaking present habits. It is different from everyone being loosely bound together but doing their own thing and working towards their own agendas. The Mobilising Step is rather like the experiment with iron filings we perhaps experienced at school, with the direction of the particles being random, until a magnet was drawn over them and they all pointed in the same direction, creating their own magnetic pull.

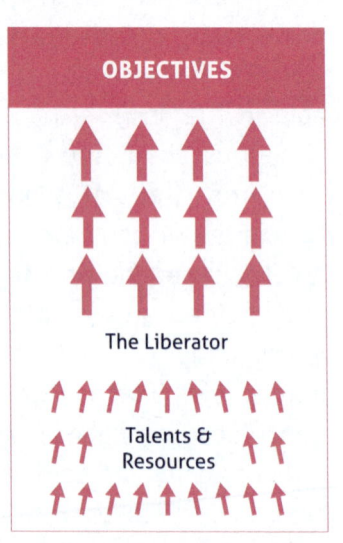

OBJECTIVES	OBJECTIVES
Talents & Resources (scattered arrows)	The Liberator — Talents & Resources (aligned arrows)

In this Mobilising Step, the Leader-Developer gets people 'on side', wanting to improve, taking increased ownership and responsibility for what they do, and doing what is right within the context of the vision.

THE 4-STEP PROCESS: VISIONING, MOBILISING, DEVELOPING, ENABLING

> **M1: Be explicit:** Specify in clear, behavioural terms, what needs to be done for successful operation, and what will be regarded as poor performance.

A skill much needed during the Mobilising Step is that of being explicit, in clear behavioural terms, about what is required, as well as what is not required. This gives team members a clear picture of what successful performance looks like and helps them improve rapidly.

Explicitness is a much undervalued and under-developed skill, in the UK at least. Often the receiver has to guess what is required of them, messages are fuzzy and confused, and what makes for successful performance is unclear, and clouded by a veneer of supposed politeness and courtesy. Being explicit is particularly important in situations of change, or where changes in behaviour are required.

Far from being patronising to the individual, as will be shown later, Explicitness is helpful and empowering in enabling individuals to succeed, when it is carried out well and appropriately.

> **M2: Get to the root of the issues:** Diagnose accurately the root cause of an individual's performance issue; identify the issue in specific behavioural terms, and the underlying reasons, and decide on a course of effective action to bring about the changes necessary.

The next important Skill at this step is to get to the root of performance issues. This is not easy to do. However, unless we get an accurate fix on the root cause of the issue, we are unlikely to make much progress. Most of us are used to analysing problems in our own discipline. Those concerning other people tend to give us far more trouble.

There is a process which helps considerably with explaining and diagnosing these issues, by looking at the difference between 'can't do' and 'won't do', and the underlying rewards or payoffs, or avoidance of consequences, people get when behaving as they do. People aren't daft – they do things for a reason, and understanding and dealing with these reasons is what matters.

We will be looking at this process, which we call the Performance Navigator, in detail in Chapter 3, because it can make such a profound and immediate difference to the way leaders work. When they start following the Performance Navigator, they find they can deal with any issue, including correcting underperformance, and moving on the good performers to an even higher level.

THE 4-STEP PROCESS: VISIONING, MOBILISING, DEVELOPING, ENABLING

> M3: Be appropriately assertive: Apply appropriately the underlying skills and attitudes of assertiveness, which are necessary for being explicit and giving feedback, but also to maintain consistency of standards and approach; exert strong leadership when necessary to prevent the team from going in different directions.

Assertiveness is not aggression and is certainly not about being passive. Assertiveness means respecting both your rights and those of the other person, staying in and operating from the I+U+ positions, and stating clearly and directly what you require, without putting the other person 'down'. To put it another way, it means standing in your own Personal Power, being grounded and self-assured while honouring the other person's point of view, thereby creating a win-win outcome. Assertiveness is particularly important during this early stage of The 4-Step Process for maintaining direction and standards, and for giving strong, clear feedback. It may be necessary to exert strong leadership at times, to prevent the team from going in different directions, and this is where engaging an appropriate level of assertion will come in.

In Chapter 4 we will be looking at how to maintain your own assertiveness, especially when giving feedback, as it seems to elude many people. Leaders we work with often mark themselves down on their ability to be appropriately assertive, so it is good to reflect on what it is like for you.

> **M4: Give empowering feedback:** Deliver feedback, both positive and negative, clearly and continuously, to reinforce positive results and correct the negative ones, in order to help the person to improve rapidly.

During this Mobilising Step especially, strong, empowering feedback is given clearly and continually to reinforce positive results and correct the negative ones, in order to help the person to improve rapidly. This is given as soon as appropriate or inappropriate behaviour is seen, and not stored up for some later occasion. The principle is to catch people doing something right, thus reinforcing that behaviour, and likewise to let them know when they are not on track. What we are talking about here are not just major changes that are spotted, but also those small important ones which, if reinforced, will cumulatively make a major difference.

Similarly, in Chapter 4, we will look at feedback in more detail, including giving feedback well, and why people sometimes don't hear praise, and why they sometimes don't hear criticism. Being appropriately assertive and giving empowering feedback go hand in hand.

THE 4-STEP PROCESS: VISIONING, MOBILISING, DEVELOPING, ENABLING

> **M5: Resiliently maintain momentum:**
> Learn rapidly from events and experiences; flexibly retain an overall vision without being thrown off course by setbacks and difficulties; keep and resiliently pursue your overall sense of direction and focus.

Situations can be both rewarding and sometimes frustrating, where progress can be slow and then quick, where individuals can improve and then regress. It requires resilience to keep going, to retain direction and your overall vision, and not be thrown off course by setbacks and difficulties. Having and retaining a strong vision and sense of mission will be what will keep you on track to make consistent progress, as will maintaining your own assertiveness capacity.

So often leaders can get bogged down with their day-to-day tasks, the constant meetings and the pressure of deadlines, and they lose their strategic focus. The 'developing' part of the Leader-Developer role gets forgotten and people suffer as a result.

To resiliently retain momentum and direction then, it is important for leaders to take time out and reflect on what is going on and pull out the learning from events. This gives them time to re-energise, re-engage with their vision and identify the next steps for them, their team and each individual within it.

Step Three: Developing

Responses from individuals are likely to vary during the Mobilising Step. Some may grasp the new direction quickly and move to achieve it, while others resist and seem unable or reluctant to change. One individual will see what needs to be done and do it well, while another may remain entirely dependent on you to be told what to do. Some may avidly want to acquire new skills and try them out, while other people can't see the point of doing so.

Also, if you are managing significant change, you will soon notice that some people adapt readily, while others need much more time. This doesn't mean that the slower people won't get there, it's likely to mean that it just needs more patience and effort. Seeing others who are through the 'boundary' and who are coping and thriving will provide role models.

When people are caught doing it right consistently, it is time to reinforce and signal the process by flexing your style to provide more participation, involvement and shared decision-making. This is the time to invite their views and suggestions, to move to a more mentoring and then Coaching style. Your behaviour and approach to the team member should be consistent with what the individual does and how they are performing.

This signals for you the need to move to the Developing Step, as the process is one which builds capacity and develops performance continually. It is underpinned by knowing each member as an individual, their strengths and weaknesses, their motivation patterns and what matters to them.

> **D1: Know individual needs and motivations:** Relate to team members as individuals; be realistic and knowledgeable about your own and others' strengths and weaknesses, be perceptive in knowing individuals' motivation patterns and needs, and be skilled in providing appropriate rewards.

The starting point here is to know your own motivation patterns and needs, for it is far too easy to assume, unthinkingly, that other people are the same as you and that what matters to you will matter to them. People are the same in that they hold much in common, but different in that all are unique individuals, each with their own patterns of needs and wants. Knowing each individual as an individual will enable you to fine-tune your approach, within the context of Situational Consistency, so that you can connect with the person appropriately.

For example, one person may rejoice in increased responsibility (which is a reward to them), while another will want the security of not taking the risk (where they currently see responsibility as a penalty, not a reward). One person may be eager for the achievement of personal mastery in their job, while another is 'just there for the money'. Yet another person may thrive on challenges, while someone else likes certainty and comfort.

Then again, some needs may be dormant, held in abeyance because more pressing needs are not being taken care of, or held in check because of the person's own expectations that such needs cannot be, or are unlikely to be, fulfilled.

What highly effective Leader-Developers are able to do is to become aware of people's individual motivation patterns and needs, and connect with them. But they do more than that, at least the Transformational ones do. They bring out and work with the internal sources of motivation the individual has, not just the external motivator of direct rewards. People start to motivate themselves and take increasing personal responsibility for what becomes their own goals of developing higher performance. Instead of 'push', the approach then becomes to 'pull', with the Leader-Developer flexing their style appropriately. This is what development and the Developing Step is all about.

In Chapter 5, ways of reviewing and understanding individual motivation patterns, including your own, will be more comprehensively explained.

> **D2: Flexibly adapt style:** Deal with individuals on the basis of what they do, not who they are; everyone knows clearly where they stand and that particular behaviours are responded to inconsistent, particular ways; be Situationally Consistent by flexibly adapting style to deal with various levels of performance and commitment to overall vision.

Participation and trust are important sources of reward and give impetus for the individual's capability, self-esteem and confidence to flower and grow.

With other people, where progress is slower, you may still need to apply close supervision and be explicit and directive in what is to be done and how. When such people make progress, you can then flex your style, treating everyone consistently according to what they do, not who they are, so that everyone knows clearly where they stand and that particular behaviours are responded to in consistent, particular ways. As flexing style, or Situational Consistency, is a key skill of Leader-Developers, and often a tricky concept to grasp, we look at it more closely in Chapter 5.

> **D3: Generate continuous improvement:** Accept responsibility for mistakes, know that they will happen occasionally; deal with them as learning opportunities; make consistent judgements about how much to become personally involved; and concentrate on problem-resolution rather than apportioning blame as you drive for continuous improvement.

This Skill is about establishing, with the individual, continuous improvement as a way of life, so that it becomes a habit. Here, the way you deal with and accept responsibility for mistakes becomes crucial, for it is akin to being a hinge point in the process. If you react as though you didn't really believe they could do it, and grab back direction through command and control, people will realise quickly that it is a game after all and you don't really trust them. If, however, you deal with the mistake as a learning opportunity, restoring confidence where necessary, then people will realise that you are for real and will be encouraged to progress further. It also builds trust and support in the relationship.

Of course, it is a different situation if the mistake is due to carelessness, lack of effort, or because the person doesn't want to or can't be bothered to do what is required. We are back to diagnosing performance issues. In such cases, where it is not a genuine mistake, reprimands are appropriate. As part of Situational Consistency, too, it is sometimes appropriate to adjust your style to a more directive one if the person is not yet capable or willing to do what is required, but the way you handle the situation will be a real marker for the future.

It is also easy and tempting to pause at this stage. After all, you have achieved a lot. You have created movement and have made a difference, with people now on side and performing more effectively. But don't stop, keep the continuous improvement going until it comes to its full fruition, for the best is yet to come.

Step Four: Enabling

> 'Begin with the end in mind.'
> — Stephen R Covey

This is the fruition step. The step at which, when completed through the facilitation of the Leader-Developer, individuals and groups have not only The Skills and knowledge to do what is required well but the will and confidence to do so. They will be operating with Responsible Initiative, in fact, being appropriately self-directing, not only with the immediate tasks but in a way where they take increasing ownership of their own continued learning to achieve personal mastery. It involves a new quality of partnership between the individuals concerned and the supporting Leader-Developer.

THE LIBERATOR

Self-direction and Responsible Initiative

Self-directing people take Responsible Initiative in managing their own situations and in creating their own success. We call them *The Pioneer*. When they see a problem, they take responsibility for ensuring it is dealt with, working out possible solutions and agreeing them, and promoting the right course of action, while taking other people's needs into account. They are effective high 'can-do' people.

This contrasts sharply with the Dependent or Counter-Dependent behaviour (where initiative is often used irresponsibly) which you may well have experienced in the journey through The 4-Step Process to this Step. Dependent people always want to be told what to do and have problems solved for them (low 'can-do'), while Counter-Dependent people are difficult to control and are dangerously unreliable, using initiative irresponsibly in a way in which they are unconcerned about or don't think through the consequences of what they do.

The Process is directed not just towards The Skills and knowledge, but also how these are applied in a self-sustaining, self-directing way. It parallels the stages of development of people as people, from childhood to a fully mature, capable and well-functioning person. The relevance is that because of the way people have often been managed at work, particularly where the style has been of a heavily 'command

THE 4-STEP PROCESS: VISIONING, MOBILISING, DEVELOPING, ENABLING

and control' or 'paternalistic' nature, or the culture has been power or role-based, people can become habituated to Dependency or Counter-Dependency.

Dependency	Being directed, nurtured and sustained by others
Counter-Dependency	Being rebellious, taking irresponsible initiative, being preoccupied with self
Independency	Taking care of self, becoming inner-directed and self-reliant, thinking own thoughts, making own decisions
Interdependency	Being self-reliant, proactive and capable, but also being able to join with other people and share resources productively

Dependency to Interdependency Model

Therefore, 'beginning with the end in mind' means developing the habits and attitudes of Responsible Initiative, or to put it another way, where people become at least Independent and preferably Interdependent.

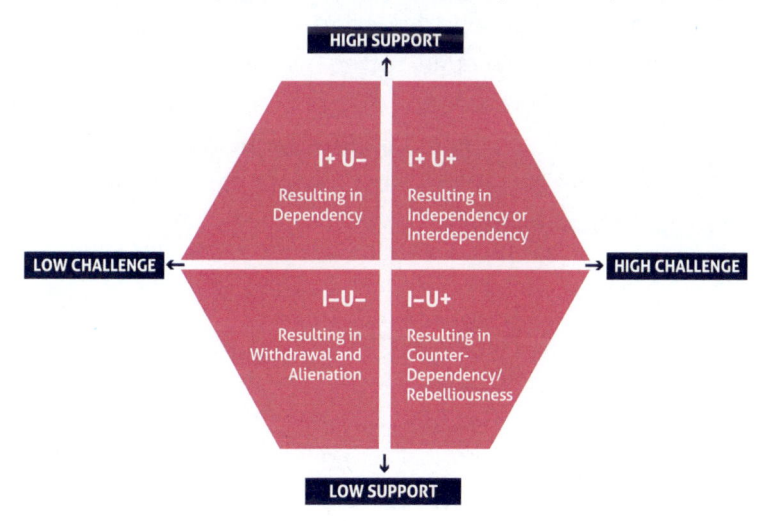

HIGH SUPPORT

I+ U−
Resulting in Dependency

I+ U+
Resulting in Independency or Interdependency

LOW CHALLENGE ← → **HIGH CHALLENGE**

I−U−
Resulting in Withdrawal and Alienation

I−U+
Resulting in Counter-Dependency/ Rebelliousness

LOW SUPPORT

We are back again to the underlying mindsets of High Challenge-High Support and I'm OK-You're OK (I+U+).

Why is this necessary and desirable? Firstly, you are unlikely to create a high-performing team without operating with these mindsets. It can be argued, of course, that in highly structured roles, or where the work is routine, being self-directing and using Responsible Initiative is not necessary. Such arguments are doubtful and, anyway, such roles are becoming increasingly rare. Secondly, because in the end it frees you, the Leader-Developer, up to apply your energies more fruitfully, rather than being overwhelmed by dealing with immediate problems.

In this fast-moving world, people are increasingly required to move from the comfortable and firm ground of the known, to cope with changing demands and requirements. This involves using their own judgement in applying new and lesser-known areas of skill and knowledge, often in situations where there are no prescribed answers, and where they have to use Responsible Initiative in judging the right course of action. This is how people can give you a competitive advantage.

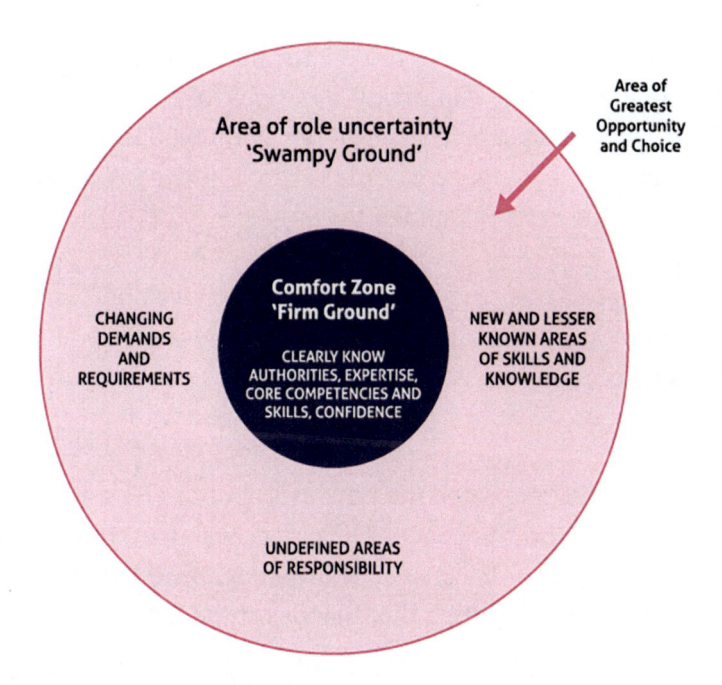

THE 4-STEP PROCESS: VISIONING, MOBILISING, DEVELOPING, ENABLING

Diagram: Concentric circles showing "Comfort Zone 'Firm Ground'" (CLEARLY KNOW AUTHORITIES, EXPERTISE, CORE COMPETENCIES AND SKILLS, CONFIDENCE) at centre, surrounded by "Area of role uncertainty 'Swampy Ground'" with labels: CHANGING DEMANDS AND REQUIREMENTS, NEW AND LESSER KNOWN AREAS OF SKILLS AND KNOWLEDGE, UNDEFINED AREAS OF RESPONSIBILITY, and an arrow pointing to "Area of Greatest Opportunity and Choice".

We call this stage the Enabling one because it rarely happens by itself. It is what Leader-Developers believe in and do that causes this to happen.

> E1: Empower team members: Build each team member's capability, will and confidence; actively reinforce achievements and enhance performance and task ownership through mentoring and coaching.

This is not leaving someone exposed to failure by leaving them to their own devices. Empowerment only comes after preparing them with the necessary skills and knowledge, reinforcing their will to succeed, and allowing people to try things out with increasing participation and involvement so their judgement and confidence are enhanced.

During all this, the style the Leader-Developer uses changes, becoming much less directive and working with the person more on a 'partnership' basis than a 'tell' one.

This is the time when the person is about to fly solo, so to speak, and the Leader-Developer will need to have the generosity to 'let go', and demonstrate trust and confidence by getting their hands off the controls.

> **E2: Delegate task ownership:** Judge when individuals are ready to manage tasks by themselves, even though they may not recognise this; delegate authority while retaining responsibility if things go wrong; be prepared to let people make their own decisions to carry out the task their own way; keep an eye on things at a discreet distance and only intervene when the situation goes badly wrong.

Delegation is both a state of mind and an action. When we talk about delegation at this point, it is more about

THE 4-STEP PROCESS: VISIONING, MOBILISING, DEVELOPING, ENABLING

The Mindset involved. It is the art of assigning authority and ownership for the completion of a task or specific activities to one of your team, once you have helped them to develop their skill and will to do the task... you know they will act with Responsible Initiative. For example, you might choose to delegate authority to make expenditures without direct approval from you, at least up to a stipulated amount.

Delegation is a step, a major and fundamental one, in the direction of empowerment, which is wide and more embracing than delegating particular tasks. For, with empowerment, the person is given the power to use their own judgement, and take risks themselves, as they develop further. It requires the willingness to share power, and to do so effectively, on the part of both the Leader-Developer and team member.

The rationale for delegation and empowerment is quite straightforward and simple. With delegation, at its most basic, the rationale is that no leader can personally accomplish or completely supervise all the organisations' or departments' tasks. To think otherwise is to fall into the trap of the old 'command and control' school of thought. Appropriate delegation frees the leader up to concentrate on issues where their attention is best spent, as well as providing others with growth, development and rewards.

To get a better idea of what delegation is, it is useful to look at what it is not. Delegation is not abdication in

THE LIBERATOR

the sense of simply giving people jobs to do and telling them to get them done. If this kind of approach is taken you are unlikely to get the results that you want, because you are expecting people to guess what you want. Here, Explicitness about the end results – the 'whats' – matter greatly if you want the person to succeed; the 'hows' of going about it is what is gifted to the team member. Likewise, the Leader-Developer does not lose responsibility for the end results; they are accountable for what occurs, just as they are responsible for maintaining support throughout.

A surprising number of Leader-Developers experience difficulty, reluctance and discomfort in moving into delegation. The barriers to delegation which they express, offered here as a rationalisation, include the following. Ask yourself which of these might apply to you:

- I can do it better myself.
- My people just aren't capable enough.
- It takes too much time to explain what I want done.
- If it goes wrong, I'll still be accountable.
- Delegation reduces my own authority.
- I'll be shown up if they do too good a job.
- My people prefer that I make the decisions.

THE 4-STEP PROCESS: VISIONING, MOBILISING, DEVELOPING, ENABLING

- Team members want to avoid responsibility (at work at least).

The real reasons for being unwilling to delegate are often because:

- I'm insufficiently organised or too inflexible to delegate efficiently
- I don't want to lose control
- I like being the expert and the one people come to

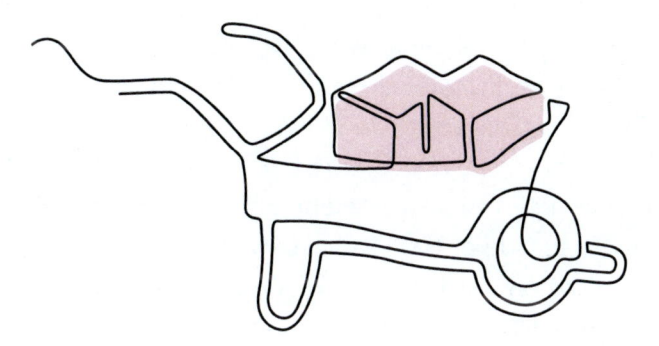

E3: Provide continued support: Continue to provide support, encouragement and reinforcement; sustain and further develop the team's high performance; focus on pulling them from good to outstanding.

When a task or tasks are delegated, the Leader-Developer's job is not done, they still need to 'be there' for the other person, providing continued support, encouragement, recognition and further development. One reason for this is that there will be other tasks that can increasingly be handed over, leading eventually to full empowerment and Interdependence. The other is that it causes and provides the relationship necessary for people to continue to both give their best and develop and grow.

This relationship requires building a level of trust between the two people: the Leader-Developer trusting the individual who has demonstrated that they can be invested in, and the individual trusting the Leader-Developer and knowing they are on their side. Such trust needs to be invested wholeheartedly by the Leader-Developer. If abused, the High Challenge side of the Leader-Developer will confront the situation, for trust involves mutuality and shared responsibility.

The manner is one of 'support and verify', not to catch the individual out, but to support their success, reinforcing it so that success through the full exercise of Responsible Initiative becomes the set of working habits.

The best Leader-Developers enable and empower others. On the other hand, leaders who enjoy having

Dependent followers, like parents who exercise power over their Dependent children, cannot foster working relationships that will enable partnership and empowerment. They like to keep their people 'Sapped' rather than 'Zapping' them through a High Challenge-High Support approach, as William C Byham describes it in *Zapp! The Lightning of Empowerment* (1999).

SAPPED	ZAPPED
Your job belongs to the company	Your job belongs to you
You are just doing whatever you are told	You are responsible
Your job doesn't really matter	Your job counts for something
You don't know how well you are doing	You know where you stand
You always have to keep your mouth shut	You have some say in how things are done
Your job is something different from who you are	Your job is just part of who you are
You have little or no control over your work	You have some control over your work

Adapted from William C Byham, Zapp! The Lightning Of Empowerment, *pp55-56*

Summing up The 4-Step Process and 15 Skills

So, this is The Process of *The Liberator* and The Skills involved, all of which are underpinned by the accompanying Mindset of High Challenge-High Support. The Skills are a mixture of those which are well known, and possibly well developed, and others which are less well known and not practised so much. You will be able to conduct your own 'MOT test', as it were, on your current skills, perhaps using the instruments provided, and through feedback from your own leader and members of your team. In this way, you can decide how to best focus your development energy. In the chapters that follow, some of the more under-developed Skills will be dealt with in more detail.

What matters, too, is how The Skills are used in combination. They are not exclusive to just one of the stages, they intertwine and reinforce each other throughout – getting to the root of issues is a skill, for example, which is of use during the Developing and Enabling Steps, as well as the Mobilising Step. The 4-Step Process also gives a structured and consistent way of going about things so that direction and momentum are maintained, particularly as different individuals will go through it at different speeds. Some people may have reached the Enabling Step while others are still at the Mobilising Step, for example. Others may be at different stages for the differing tasks which make up their job.

Looking at The Skills and characteristics of the effective Leader-Developer, some are Transactional ones, others are Transformational ones.

SUMMING UP THE 4-STEP PROCESS AND 15 SKILLS

Transformational Skills are those which feature in the Developing and Enabling Steps of The 4-Step Process, plus that part of Visioning which sees people performing at their best and fulfilling their true performance potential. Although the term 'Transformational Leader' sounds as though heroic qualities are required, achieving such sustained high performance and success is well within the grasp of the Leader-Developers who care enough to put themselves out to make it all happen. Of course, this involves developing and maintaining the attitudes and skills required within The 4-Step Process.

It is the Transformational Leaders who achieve the Enabling Step with their people. This is not to minimise the Transactional Skills – much can be achieved with these alone. But, above all, Transformational Leaders 'begin with the end in mind', seeing their people operating at their best and being the best they can be... what they 'vision' they cause to happen.

THE LIBERATOR

1.	VISIONING STEP	
V1	Have authentic personal style	Project and consistently hold a clear personal style and a strong sense of who you are and what you stand for, which is clearly visible to others
V2	Stand back and watch	Listen and question effectively to establish facts and information; consult with others to get views; perceptively observe differences between what is said and done, and where improvements can be made
V3	Decide right course of action	Analyse the present situation accurately by seeing above the waves; sift information and form views without jumping to conclusions; manage complexity without becoming submerged by it and decide the right course of action
V4	Set clear vision	Create your vision with a clear sense of direction, transmit enthusiasm for and commitment to it; vision everyone in the team performing at their very best and being the best they can be
2. MOBILISING STEP		
M1	Be explicit	Specify in clear, behavioural terms, what needs to be done for successful operation, and what will be regarded as poor performance
M2	Get to the root of issues	Diagnose accurately the root cause of an individual's performance issue; identify the issue in specific behavioural terms, and the underlying reasons, and decide on a course of effective action to bring about the changes necessary
M3	Be appropriately assertive	Apply appropriately the underlying skills and attitudes of assertiveness, necessary for being explicit and giving feedback, but also to maintain consistency of standards and approach; exert strong leadership when necessary to prevent the team going in different directions
M4	Give empowering feedback	Deliver feedback, both positive and negative, clearly and continuously to reinforce positive results and correct the negative ones, in order to help the person to improve rapidly
M5	Resiliently maintain momentum	Learn rapidly from events and experiences; flexibly retain overall vision, without being thrown off course by setbacks and difficulties; keep and resiliently pursue your overall sense of direction and focus

	3. DEVELOPING STEP	
D1	Know individual needs and motivations	Relate to team members as individuals; be realistic and knowledgeable about own and others' strengths and weaknesses; perceptive in knowing individuals' motivation patterns and needs, and skilled in providing appropriate rewards
D2	Flexibly adapt style	Deal with individuals on the basis of what they do, not who they are; everyone knows clearly where they stand and that particular behaviours are responded to in consistent, particular ways; be situationally consistent by flexibly adapting style to deal with various levels of performance and commitment to overall vision
D3	Generate continuous improvement	Accept responsibility for mistakes, know that they will happen occasionally; deal with them as learning opportunities; make consistent judgements about how much to become personally involved; concentrate on problem resolution rather than apportioning blame as you drive for continuous improvement
	4. ENABLING STEP	
E1	Empower team members	Build each team member's capability, will and confidence; actively reinforce achievements and enhance performance and task ownership through mentoring and coaching
E2	Delegate task ownership	Judge when individuals are ready to manage tasks by themselves, even though they may not recognise this; delegate authority while retaining responsibility if things go wrong; be prepared to let people make their own decisions to carry out the task their own way; keep an eye on things at a discreet distance and only intervene when the situation goes badly wrong
E3	Provide continued support	Continue to provide support, encouragement and reinforcement; sustain and further develop team's high performance; focus on pulling them from good to outstanding

Chapter summary

The Liberator:

- Follows a simple 4-Step Process, underpinned and reinforced by The Mindset and beliefs of High Challenge-High Support.

- The 4-Steps are:
  - 1: Visioning
  - 2: Mobilising
  - 3: Developing
  - 4: Enabling

- Works to the principle of 'begin with the end in mind' and their Vision invariably includes, in their own words, seeing people operating at their best and becoming the best they can be.

- Sees their role in The 4-Step Process as enabling people to move on from Dependency, and instead becoming Interdependent and operating with Responsible Initiative.

- Understands the difference between management and leadership and elects to be a Leader-Developer, recognising that they are part of the situation, and they define that situation. This means they cause things to happen.

SUMMING UP THE 4-STEP PROCESS AND 15 SKILLS

- Uses the necessary Transactional Skills, and they also use Transformational ones. They motivate people to achieve and develop much more than was originally thought possible, by connecting people to the energy of their own internal motivation and needs so that they become self-directing.

- Works on a both/and basis of Vision and action: 'Vision without action is just a dream; action without vision is meaningless and boring; vision with action can change the world'.

- Knows that successful completion of The 4-Step Process is a step-by-step, little-and-often, cumulative process, with people proceeding through it at different rates, and the Leader-Developer flexes their style according to where people are in The 4-Step Process.

- Operates a set of key Skills involved at each step. Some of these Skills are well known and are likely to be well developed. Others are less well known and are likely to need to be developed (which we move onto in the next chapter).

- Appreciates The Skills are best applied as an integrated whole. They know effective Leader-Developers have strong Developing and Enabling Skills as well as Visioning and Mobilising ones, set within the context of High Challenge-High Support.

3

THE SKILLS: MOBILISING STEP - UNDER-DEVELOPED SKILLS

M1: Be Explicit
The art of Explicitness
The Onion Model
The Skills of Explicitness and when to use them
M2: Get to the Root of Issues
Why people behave as they do
Diagnosing the root cause of performance issues
Performance Navigator
Chapter summary

'Clients do not come first, employees come first. If you take care of your employees, they will take care of your clients.'
— Richard Branson

M1: Be Explicit

Specify in clear, behavioural terms, what needs to be done for successful operation, and what will be regarded as poor performance.

The Skill of being explicit is one of the most under-emphasised leadership skills, and often the one that leaders find most helpful when they are introduced to it. But what is it exactly, and why is it helpful?

The art of Explicitness

Imagine that you are responsible for teaching a small child to cross the road. Would you take that child to the edge of a fast motorway and say to them something like, 'The objective of the exercise is to cross the road and then return safely – now off you go and let me know how you get on'? Of course you wouldn't, the consequences don't bear thinking about! Yet this is analogous to the approach which many managers adopt when briefing their staff about what they require them to do.

The highly effective Leader-Developers we worked with, however, used well a fundamental Skill which was a basis for their success. Yet this Skill is rarely taught, rarely mentioned in management texts, and it is assumed that most people who lead groups have it. They don't or don't use it.

This is The Skill of defining and communicating in unambiguous behavioural terms exactly what performance they want, as well as clearly describing the behaviours they don't want. Leaders fail to achieve the performance they require because they haven't thought through, explicitly, what they require and/or don't communicate this explicitly. Sometimes this is done under the mistaken belief that to do so is patronising. It isn't, on the contrary, it can be particularly helpful, especially during the Mobilising Step.

The first thing to understand about Explicitness is that it focuses on behaviour, rather than the personality or values of the person. It is very much grounded in Positive Regard and Genuineness, which is always the starting point. You want each member of your team to perform rapidly, so why not tell them exactly what you need for their success and the overall team's success? And why not also explain clearly what you don't want, so they don't fall into any 'tiger traps', which would lead to everyone feeling disenchanted?

Leader-Developers are skilled at treating their people with the kind of unconditional Positive Regard and love they would give to their children. They focus on behaviour, which keeps the mind clear and focused.

What happens if you don't have this mindset, is that you can all too easily become ground down by the emotion of a situation, of someone's poor performance or attitude to work. By becoming embroiled in things in this way, managers lose their ability to focus and make rational decisions, which prevents growth in the leader and the individual staff member. Often, the only choice they feel they have is to fire them, which is easier, in their mind, than sorting out the problem.

Over the coming pages, we'll share some powerful models to help you know how to be explicit, where you need to apply this Skill, and then how to get to the root of issues with purpose and clarity to help everyone achieve.

The first useful way of crystallising this is through the Onion Model.

The Onion Model

Personality, values, attitudes and behaviours

If it is necessary for an individual to increase their performance or to develop their skills in a particular area, a change is required. For some people, this change appears to be unachievable as, at first sight, it seems to require them to be something they are not, and as a result the change does not happen.

This same view can often be a barrier to the Leader-Developer who may hesitate to deliver the total message for fear of damaging sensibilities, or of expecting a total shift in someone's personality: 'I need Mark to show more initiative, but I can't tell him as he's not that sort of person.'

The Onion Model illustrates how people are made up of different layers, and how, by focusing on the required changes to behaviour, which make up the outer layers of the onion, it makes the message much more effective and easier to give. It is also easier for the recipient to take in and act on.

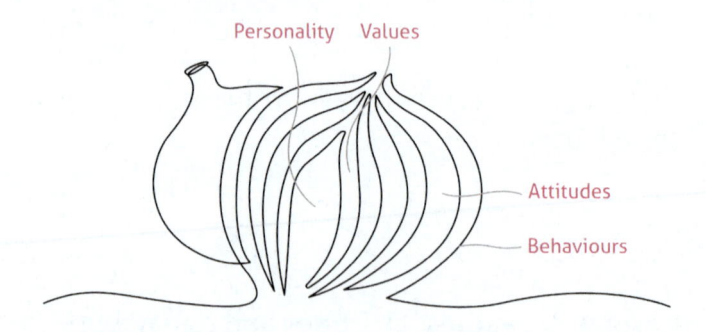

Personality
Values
Attitudes
Behaviours

Personality: At the core of a person is their personality. This is largely set in adults, and it is not within the Leader-Developer's rights or abilities to try to change someone's personality. Personality is someone's inner being, the integral self. To criticise this inner being is experienced as attacking the person and will provoke a negative and unproductive response.

Values: These are a person's deep-seated beliefs which are relatively enduring and connected with their personality. They are the way the person makes sense of the world and provide an essential modus operandi for the way they lead their life. They, too, form an integral part of the person's being.

Values are not readily changed in the normal course of events. Where there is disagreement between two people, it will not be resolved by one trying to change the other's values. Again, this will be experienced as attacking the person's integral self and will result in defensiveness and resistance.

An underlying approach to take when dealing with others is that of having Positive Regard for them as individuals. This means accepting, respecting and valuing the integral self of the other person. It means holding and projecting the view that the other person is OK and having a positive belief in them as a person. If this is not the case, then the person will feel 'written off' or 'disliked', instead of being valued.

The outer layers of the Onion Model are attitudes and behaviours. These are more to do with what an individual actually says and does, rather than who they are.

It is at this level that problems can be addressed, and changes more readily effected.

Attitudes: Attitudes are the underlying beliefs or approaches to work and life which underpin behaviour. They are less deep-rooted than values and can change. For example, a team member might have an attitude about a particular type of work, stemming from their own belief that it is of little importance or not valued. Their attitude can change completely, in this instance, if someone demonstrates why this work is important and how it benefits the organisation.

The Stephen Covey example used at the beginning of Chapter 1 – Part 2: The Mindset, is a prime example of how your attitude can change in an instant.

Behaviours: This is what people actually do, how they handle clients, brief their teams, appraise their staff, and so on. Behaviours are visible to all, and the acquisition of the right behaviours appropriate to the situation, underpinned by supporting attitudes, is what leads to improved performance.

It is important then to concentrate on the behaviours and attitudes displayed by the team member. You are commenting on what they do, not who they are.

The attitude of Positive Regard is key; it helps reinforce that underneath the behaviours leading to poor performance there is a person to be valued and who deserves Explicitness to allow them to make the changes required.

The Skills of Explicitness and when to use them

Explicitness, then, is defining, and specifying in explicit behavioural terms, what is required, so that the person has a clear mental picture of the actions, behaviour and outputs that:

- Are required for effective performance
- Lead to poor performance and are unhelpful

These definitions of expected behaviour are specific and not general or ambiguous.

Phrases such as 'You need to adopt a more positive attitude' or 'You need to work on your client relations' are not helpful. They leave the recipient with a plethora of possible meanings and actions to take, only one of which is going to address the problem as it is actually seen by the Leader-Developer.

The key to Explicitness is the ability to define, in unambiguous behavioural terms, exactly what performance is positive and to be encouraged, and what is a problem and needs to be changed.

To illustrate the point, the following two scenarios show two possible approaches to dealing with the same situation:

Scenario One: 'One problem area we need to look at is your communication with your colleagues. You really need to keep them in the picture more so there are no nasty surprises lurking. The X project is a case in point, I'm sure you know what I mean.'

Scenario Two: 'One area I need to tell you about that is causing me problems is your communication with me and others working with you on projects. I'd like to use the X project as an example of what I mean.

'Your initial briefing to us was fine – it had clear terms of reference and deadlines and our individual responsibilities were clearly delineated. I found that particularly helpful.

'However, when the deadline was brought forward, you didn't tell me. This caused problems with resources and meant that I had to drop two options that might have been useful to the client. I know that deadlines shift, but what would help next time would be if you called a short meeting as soon as you hear of a change, and ensure that we all hear the same message and can re-schedule the work together.

'There is one other point I would like to mention that came out of the X project. At the meeting when we

M1: BE EXPLICIT

discussed contingencies, you seemed not to be listening. You were continually looking at your watch and left the meeting twice to answer calls on your phone. Contingency plans were agreed but none of us felt that you fully understood the implications or the costs. It would have been more helpful for you to summarise what was said and produce a short note detailing the changes so that we could be confident we were all proceeding to the same revised schedule.'

Scenario Two is far more likely to achieve the desired results as specific behavioural issues were addressed. The recipient is clear about what they had done to cause the problem and what they need to do in the future. Although Scenario Two is longer, it is surprising how often being explicit takes less time in the long run.

Explicitness gives clarity. It also gives choice because the issues are made clear. The clarity and directness give it a power which, by itself, is likely to produce results. However, it may be that this power inhibits people from being explicit, along with a possible confusion that personality and values are part of the arena. They are not. The arena is behaviour only, and being specific about what is required is legitimate, helpful and inoffensive when delivered properly.

The way it is delivered has to be from the I+U+ position of two adults dealing with a situation. Even when the behaviour is one which needs to be corrected, it is not the person who is at fault, they are still OK, the

THE LIBERATOR

issue is their behaviour, on this occasion. You still have Positive Regard for them, demonstrably so in that you are Genuine in being clear about what you mean and that you mean what you say.

Explicitness is particularly useful in the initial stage of the process where there needs to be emphasis on what needs to be done and how to do it. In the latter stages of The Process, the emphasis will change; clarity on 'the what' is still required, but a lot more discretion and participation is encouraged with the how.

Explicitness too is the starting point for getting to the root of performance issues, and hopefully nipping them in the bud before they become a serious problem. We will be looking at the powerful Performance Navigator in the next section, to help with this.

However, before moving on to the Performance Navigator, there is some important work to do first to prepare. This next model will help you start being explicit when thinking about a performance issue. Even if you are thinking about a good performer, you'll still want to move them to the next level. The clearer you can be about how you see them doing this, the more you will help them.

This model is called the Change Sheet. The concept is simple, and helps you build rigour into your thinking about people. It helps you get out of your own way and write down, explicitly, what the performance

M1: BE EXPLICIT

issue is, how this manifests as behaviour, and what their behaviour would look like if they were performing brilliantly.

If you can think of an issue where performance needs improving, either in yourself or in someone else, first write down on the Change Sheet below what the issue is, or, in other words, what are we actually talking about?

Then write down what the current undesirable behaviours are. Keep them as explicit as possible. For example, rather than saying 'They have a bad attitude', write down the behaviours the person is displaying that make you believe they have a bad attitude. Is it their facial expressions, the way they speak to people, their timekeeping or mistakes in their work, for instance?

If the issue is with you and the performance issue is, say, that you are not getting enough sleep, how does this present itself in undesirable behaviour? Maybe you stay up scrolling through your social media or watching TV?

When you have written your list of present undesirable behaviours, close your eyes and imagine the person performing brilliantly. You are thinking about their future desirable behaviour. Now write this down in the right-hand column as explicitly as you can. In the sleep example above, you might put 'Be in bed by 10pm on five nights a week, and on those five nights, leave the phone in a different room by 9.30pm'.

THE LIBERATOR

Complete the Change Sheet now to prepare you for the next session and see the difference this makes to your sense of peace.

Performance issue:	
Present Undesirable Behaviours (Less of required)	**Future Desirable Behaviours (More of required)**

'The task of leadership is not to put greatness into people, but to elicit it, for the greatness is already there.'
— John Buchan

M2: Get to the Root of Issues

Diagnose accurately the root cause of an individual's performance issue; identify the issue in specific behavioural terms, and the underlying reasons, and decide on a course of effective action to bring about the changes necessary.

Why people behave as they do

Most of us have learned to become adept at diagnosing performance issues in our area of technical or specialist expertise. If a piece of equipment is not working properly, or a system is failing, or there are persistent quality problems, what we do is to diagnose the root cause of such problems. We know that to solve the problem we have to get to the root of the issue – there is no point in proceeding otherwise, and we have help available in diagnosing these types of problems using a range of techniques – eg brainstorming, diagrams, flow charts, technical manuals, etc.

When it comes to diagnosing 'people' problems, however, we are often much less adept, and tend to resort to a level of generalisation such as saying, 'It's an attitude problem' or a 'training/development issue'. This is not terribly accurate or helpful in moving things forward. What is necessary is a way of identifying what the problem really is and the reasons for it occurring.

The difficulty may be that people are seen as much more complicated and unpredictable than 'things' (they are, thank goodness), but there are still ways of understanding what is going on and why. This can be done without getting immersed too deeply in the mystical realms of psychology, rather remaining in the arena of behaviour and attitudes.

People aren't daft – they do things for a reason. Identifying the reason is the most important part of being able to get to the root of the issue. In starting to explore the source of these reasons, there is an old Hungarian fable which has much to teach us.

> A man was out fishing in a boat on a lake. It was a beautiful day, and the fisherman was feeling pleased with the world. There was a tug on his line, and when he reeled it in there was a snake – and the snake had a live frog in its mouth.
>
> Feeling sorry for the frog, the fisherman took it from the snake and threw the frog back into the water. Then he felt that perhaps that

had not been fair on the snake, so he looked around the boat to see what he could give the snake. All he had was a flask of brandy, so he gave the snake a slug of brandy and then threw the snake back in the water.

Ten seconds later, there was a loud knocking on the side of the boat, and there was the snake again – this time with two frogs in its mouth.

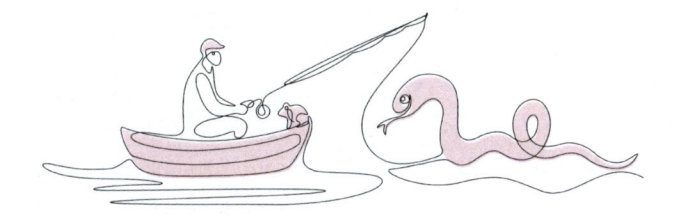

The point of this story is that:

- What gets rewarded gets done
- You get more of the behaviours you reward
- It is easy to inadvertently reward the wrong thing!

Diagnosing the root cause of performance issues

People tend to do things they find rewarding, and avoid doing things where there is a negative consequence or payoff for them. The reason we do or don't do something is much influenced by the perceived rewards, or penalties, which flow from our actions. Yet, as leaders, we are often guilty of rewarding inappropriate behaviour, such as not giving the worst jobs to those who complain most, but instead to those who complain least; giving the most attention to people who perform poorly and not those who perform highly, or 'punishing' someone for under-spending their budget by inappropriately reducing their budget the following year.

Other key factors in getting to the root of issues are whether the person knows clearly what is expected (Explicitness), and whether they are doing what they are doing because they don't have the skills and knowledge required (Can't Do), or whether they do have the capability but choose not to exercise it (Won't Do). These are the basic tools for diagnosing performance issues.

It helps, though, to have a disciplined process to follow – a flowchart in fact, which we call the Performance Navigator. Sometimes there is a measure of stress in the situation, and when this is the case it becomes even more important to have a clear, rational way to diagnose what is going on. It is rather like dealing with a failed diesel engine in a boat at sea – the law seems to be that engines break down when you need them most. It is so easy to get confused, or jump to the wrong conclusion, to start stripping the engine down

M2: GET TO THE ROOT OF ISSUES

perhaps, when a glance at the diagnostic flow chart in the owner's manual gives a logical sequence to work to – 'check to see if there is fuel in the tank' is better done before stripping the engine down than afterwards. Of course, experienced mechanics become so familiar with the process that they don't have to use the manual – so it will be for you, if you follow the process we are suggesting.

Initially, though, it is useful to build up your diagnostic skills by adopting the discipline of working through the Performance Navigator step-by-step, and always starting in Box 1, rather than in the middle of the chart. Eventually, it will become part of you, and because your subsequent action will be based on an accurate diagnosis, you will become highly effective in resolving performance issues.

The approach is not just confined to remedying poor performance, it is equally valuable in further developing already good performance or helping someone through transition and change. One important point is the need to take early, rather than late, action when you see a performance issue developing. The risk with not intervening early is that new habits can form, or the inappropriate behaviour becomes entrenched, making it much more difficult to deal with and resolve later on.

We will be dealing with the rewards and negative consequences, or penalties, available to the Leader-Developer of high performance in Chapter 4.

What is important, at this stage, is to stress that we are not talking about pots of gold, or whips (usually unavailable to the modern leader anyway), but instead a rich source of subtle and lighter approaches, as the following example will illustrate.

> **CASE STUDY: JANE**
>
> Jane, a practice manager in a small consultancy practice, had no direct authority over Tim, one of the partners. At the end of each month, Jane had to deal with the expenses submitted by each partner. The problem she had was that Tim regularly sent in his expenses several weeks late. Jane decided to do something about this.
>
> She talked to Tim and told him that his lateness was causing her a problem. Tim's attention was immediately caught because he got on well with Jane. Then she told him that his lateness was interrupting the time she was able to spend with her children. Again, this had a strong effect because Tim had children the same age as Jane's, and he was a strong family man. However, she knew that Tim, despite his good intentions, would still leave his expenses on the kitchen table when the sun shone, or there were more interesting things for him to do. So, she told him that Fred (another partner who Tim constantly worked with) always got his expenses in on time. That provided the real incentive.
>
> The next month end, Tim phoned Jane to see whether he had beaten Fred (who knew nothing about all this at

> the time). 'Not quite, but you're within distance,' was the reply. The next month when Tim phoned, it was the same: 'Nearly, it was close, but Fred just beat you'. The following month, Tim 'cracked' it. He got from Jane a simple card with a big gold star on it, like children are given at school, with the message 'Well done Tim, you've beaten Fred!'
>
> Tim's expenses have never since been sent to Jane significantly late.

This story also illustrates one other factor concerning performance. Inconvenience to the other person, even when that other person is liked and respected, is usually not a sufficient spur to act to remove such inconvenience for the other person. The intentions may be good, but often the action does not consistently follow through. It is only when the inconvenience is experienced by the person not performing as required, such as through the lack of reward or the experiencing of penalties, that action starts to happen.

At this stage, though, we will concentrate on getting to the root of the particular performance issue, using the following Performance Navigator and exploring each step in the process.

Ali Stewart & Co — The Liberator

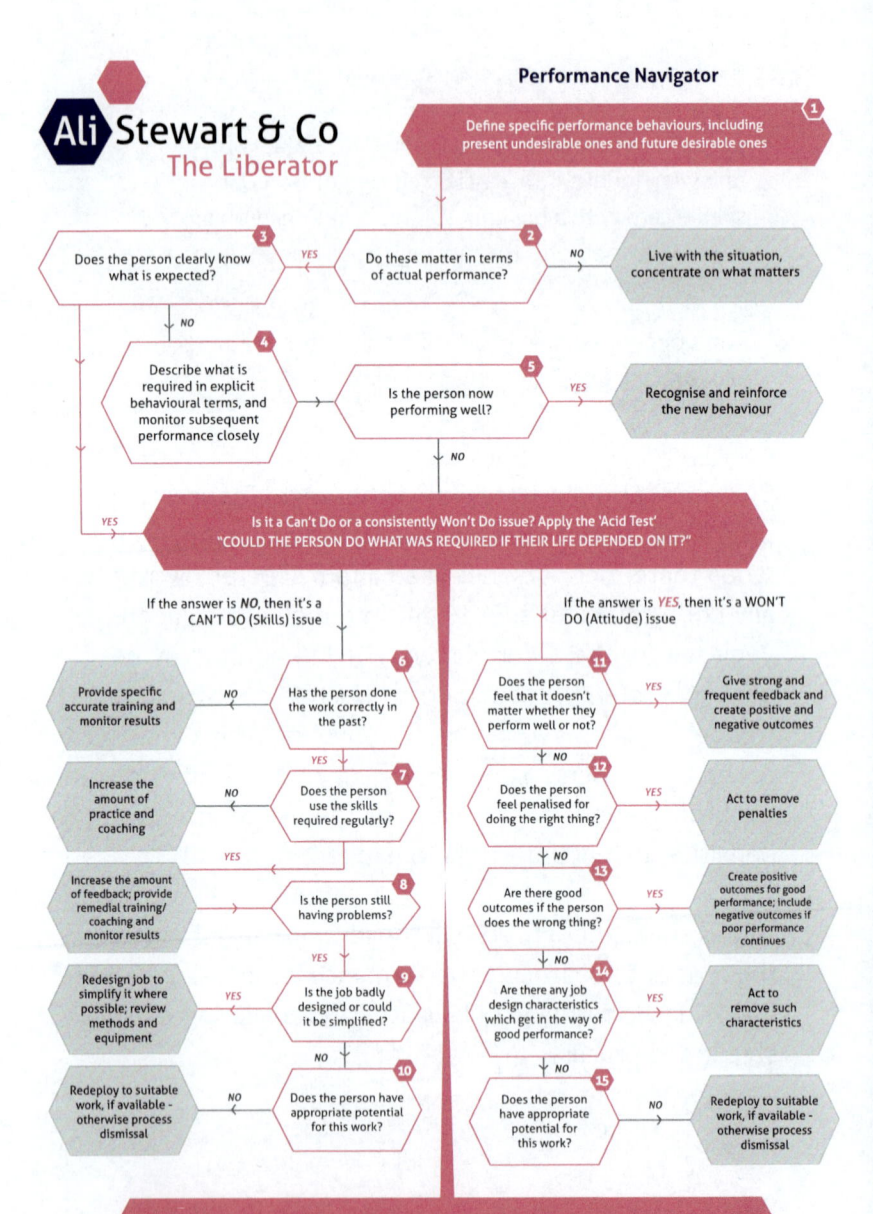

Performance Navigator

1. Define specific performance behaviours, including present undesirable ones and future desirable ones

2. Do these matter in terms of actual performance?
- **NO** → Live with the situation, concentrate on what matters
- **YES** ↓

3. Does the person clearly know what is expected?
- **YES** → (to 5)
- **NO** ↓

4. Describe what is required in explicit behavioural terms, and monitor subsequent performance closely

5. Is the person now performing well?
- **YES** → Recognise and reinforce the new behaviour
- **NO** ↓

Is it a Can't Do or a consistently Won't Do issue? Apply the 'Acid Test'
"COULD THE PERSON DO WHAT WAS REQUIRED IF THEIR LIFE DEPENDED ON IT?"

If the answer is NO, then it's a CAN'T DO (Skills) issue

6. Has the person done the work correctly in the past?
- **NO** → Provide specific accurate training and monitor results
- **YES** ↓

7. Does the person use the skills required regularly?
- **NO** → Increase the amount of practice and coaching
- **YES** ↓

8. Is the person still having problems?
- **YES** → Increase the amount of feedback; provide remedial training/coaching and monitor results
- **NO** ↓

9. Is the job badly designed or could it be simplified?
- **YES** → Redesign job to simplify it where possible; review methods and equipment
- **NO** ↓

10. Does the person have appropriate potential for this work?
- **NO** → Redeploy to suitable work, if available - otherwise process dismissal

If the answer is YES, then it's a WON'T DO (Attitude) issue

11. Does the person feel that it doesn't matter whether they perform well or not?
- **YES** → Give strong and frequent feedback and create positive and negative outcomes
- **NO** ↓

12. Does the person feel penalised for doing the right thing?
- **YES** → Act to remove penalties
- **NO** ↓

13. Are there good outcomes if the person does the wrong thing?
- **YES** → Create positive outcomes for good performance; include negative outcomes if poor performance continues
- **NO** ↓

14. Are there any job design characteristics which get in the way of good performance?
- **YES** → Act to remove such characteristics
- **NO** ↓

15. Does the person have appropriate potential for this work?
- **NO** → Redeploy to suitable work, if available - otherwise process dismissal

IDENTIFY SOLUTION, ACT ON IT AND FOLLOW THROUGH CONSISTENTLY

Performance Navigator

As we walk you through the exact process the highly effective Leader-Developers employed in our research, it might help you to have a performance issue in mind. Maybe the one you have already identified on your Change Sheet. You'll see this sets you up well for Box 1 on the chart.

Box 1: Define the specific performance behaviours, including present undesirable ones and future desirable ones

This is the essential starting position. The accuracy of the diagnosis will depend on this stage, just as a physician starts with the symptoms of an illness instead of dangerously leaping to conclusions about the nature of the illness.

For symptoms, we can read behaviours – what the person is or is not doing – defined in explicit, behavioural terms. It is the outer ring, the behaviour one of the Onion Model, that matters at this stage; it enables what is actually happening (observable facts) to be captured and identified. It is the way to unravel those sometimes seemingly intractable or complex problems and to get a handle on them so you can proceed with clarity and confidence.

We are not talking here just about poor performers. Many existing good performers could turn in an even better performance by improving in one or two areas. Other people are still developing and growing and will do so more surely and quickly with this approach. In addition, the process is useful in helping people manage change and transition, for moving through it one step at a time and successfully completing the process so that they end up more competent and capable than they were at the beginning.

Some performance issues may seem overwhelmingly large, swamping you with their very scale and seeming complexity. The way to proceed is one step at a time so that cumulatively, over time, and through reinforcement, major changes can be achieved. In these cases, it is often best to concentrate, initially, on those immediate behavioural changes which will have the greatest effect.

At first, until the process becomes an integral part of the way you work, and so that you don't get wrapped up in the emotion of the situation, it is helpful to write down the present undesirable behaviours (less of) and the future desirable ones (more of). We use the Change Sheet for this purpose, to help keep things clear and simple. You can write a Change Sheet for each performance issue and capture the corresponding behaviours which need improvement. People don't usually change their behaviour overnight. It is through a series of small steps, one change at a time.

M2: GET TO THE ROOT OF ISSUES

Going through this discipline will also concentrate your mind on getting to the essence of the issue. At the same time, it prepares you for the discussion with the individual once you have completed the diagnosis and decided your course of action.

Box 2: Do these matter in terms of actual performance?

This is where you have to be honest with yourself. It may be that the scale of the 'problem' does not matter in terms of actual performance and somehow it has got out of proportion. Take the person, for example, who produces £10K of good quality business every month, but is always a day late in submitting it. Or where the issue irritates the hell out of you personally – perhaps a speech habit or mannerism – but which really does not matter in terms of actual performance. Then again, you may occasionally find fault with the other person because, basically, they are not like you, forgetting, for the moment, that it is what they actually do – their performance and behaviour are the issue, not the person themselves.

The other side of the coin is to pretend that something does not matter when it does (to 'cop out' in fact), or to maintain that all your people are 'perfect' and are working to their full potential. This does no one any favours, not the organisation, not the individuals concerned, and certainly not you. Or it may be that one of your people is doing a good, reliable job, but wants to stay in the security of their comfort zone and not take on anything new. Is this acceptable into the future, or will it inhibit their future security or the team's performance?

The question to be answered is whether the behaviour matters in terms of high performance. If the answer is NO, then the action is for you to live with the situation, and concentrate on what does matter. If the answer is YES (which most often is the case), then the question in Box 3 must be addressed.

Box 3: Does the person clearly know what is expected?

Quite simply, if the person doesn't clearly know what is expected, then whether they succeed or not is a matter of chance. The need for the Mobilising Skills of Explicitness was described earlier; without Explicitness, in the early Steps, people are not positioned to succeed – rather they are positioned to fail. If the person does not clearly know what is expected and is not performing well because of this, then the fault and responsibility are primarily yours.

This applies even when people have work delegated to them or are working in an 'empowered' way. There is an important distinction here between knowing the standards and outputs required, and the judgements and actions an individual takes to achieve these. Both delegation and empowerment require Explicitness about standards and outputs required, even if it is mostly concerned with working to certain operating principles and values. Without this, people will be working in the dark. Mistakes, genuine ones, will happen when judgements are made and this is a part of learning. It is only when such mistakes are persistent that more remedial approaches, involving perhaps a different leadership style, come into play (see Chapter 5).

Ask yourself whether the person involved clearly knows what is expected. If the answer is YES, perhaps because you have briefed that person explicitly several times in the recent past, then you need to move on to the next stage in the Navigator. If the answer is NO, then you will need to concentrate on Box 4.

Box 4: Describe what is required in explicit, behavioural terms, and monitor subsequent performance closely

In many situations, the simple and straightforward act of describing what is required in explicit, behavioural terms, of addressing the issue firmly and assertively but with Positive Regard, and to do so early on before the situation becomes embedded, will be sufficient.

When people know what is and what is not required, and there is no discretion about it, providing they have the capability they will often quite simply deliver to these requirements – 'If that's what you want, that's what you'll get.' Of course, this only applies when the issue is addressed at the behaviour level, and not at the values or personality ones.

Where people are moving through the transition of change, such Explicitness is also helpful and enabling, for the Explicitness provides clarity and certainty, where before there may have existed only confusion and ambiguity. With development and coaching, too, it is often appropriate – the focus here being more on outputs and standards rather than how to achieve them, while with poor or inexperienced performers, there will need to be an emphasis on both outputs/standards and the behavioural 'hows' of achieving them.

The preparation done in Box 1 will prove to be valuable here. Remember that what is required will have been described in explicit behavioural terms, when the person clearly understands the actions, behaviour and outputs that are:

- Required and expected
- Not desired and are inappropriate, and
- Where these are specific, not general or ambiguous

It is not enough to leave things here. There is a need to follow through and monitor subsequent performance

M2: GET TO THE ROOT OF ISSUES

closely, not just once, but sufficiently to ensure that the person not only understands and is capable of doing what is required, but has absorbed the new learning or habits consistently into their work pattern. This leads to Box 5 in the Performance Navigator.

Box 5: Is the person now performing well?

If the answer is YES, then this needs to be recognised and reinforced through appropriate feedback (as will be discussed in Chapter 4). It may also be the time to take the next step of another incremental change or piece of development, building on the person's success thus far.

If the person is *not* now performing well – or the answer to Box 3 was YES – the issue lies at a deeper level of analysis. It means you need to move on to the 'Acid Test', which follows.

When people know what is required and their performance consistently does not reach this level, one of two sets of reasons will apply... with just occasionally a mix of the two:

1. **They CAN'T DO:** They don't have the skills/knowledge/competence required.
2. **They WON'T DO:** They don't have the will to do what is required, or choose not to – often called 'attitude'.

The 'Acid Test' then, is to analyse whether the issue is a Can't Do or Won't Do one, by asking, 'Could the person do what is required if their life depended on it?'

If the answer is NO, then it is a Skills issue.

If the answer is YES, then it is an attitude/will issue.

The majority of poor performance issues, in our experience at least, are Won't Do ones. That is, the people concerned would meet the standards required if their lives depended on it – provided they knew clearly what was expected. They could do it if they had to!

The tendency, however, is to answer the issue as a Can't Do one, maybe because it's often an easier option, maybe through being over-generous in giving the benefit of the doubt, maybe because it is too much trouble to assume anything else. Leader-Developers who have a strong inclination to Support are prone to do this, whereas those with a strong Challenge bias are more likely to assume that issues are generally Won't Do ones. This is where using the idea of the High Challenge-High Support approach is so important – to ensure that the issue is faced for what it is. Operating to this diagnostic framework, that is, the Performance Navigator, will give you the rigour to analyse, accurately, the source of the problem and then go on to resolve it.

M2: GET TO THE ROOT OF ISSUES

If the issues are in the Won't Do arena, there will be a payoff for the people concerned, either in the form of some rewards or the avoidance of perceived negative outcomes, so it is important to find out the reasons for their behaviour. As was described in the Fisherman Fable, what gets rewarded gets done, and it is easy to inadvertently reward the wrong thing, as we will see.

Firstly, though, we will follow the Can't Do route through the Performance Navigator, before looking at the Won't Do issues.

Box 6: Can't Do (Skills) issue – has the person done the work correctly in the past?

If the answer is NO, then basically the responsibility for the poor performance is yours, and the way the person is dealt with will be different to that used in a Won't Do situation, as will be described in more detail in Chapter 4.

The action is to provide specific, accurate training and to monitor the results. Training here does not necessarily mean courses; there will be a range of options available to you, including personal tuition, coaching, on-the-job instruction or arranging for someone who does the work well to teach the person. The approach, too, will need to reflect the person's general level of competence and experience. Whether you carry out the training yourself or not, you will need to monitor

145

the results, to make sure that the person is now meeting the performance required.

In one case we came across, a new appointee was knowledgeable about the product but seemed unable to sell it even though he got on famously with prospective clients who welcomed his opinion.

In order to make a sale, he had to access computer records to check prices and stock availability, but did not know how to, and was ashamed to admit it (he had previously been a director in a smaller firm which had been absorbed into the group).

When his leader had analysed the problem and realised what was going on, and given him three hours of hands-on training, the 'poor performer', within a year, became one of the top-performing salesmen in the region.

If the answer is YES, that is, the person has carried out the work correctly in the recent past and the level of performance is not sufficient, then we need to explore Box 7.

Box 7: Can't Do (Skills) issue – does the person use the skills required regularly?

Sometimes, people get rusty if the skill required is not used regularly. In this case, it is not as though

M2: GET TO THE ROOT OF ISSUES

the person can't do it, it's more a case of getting back to speed and quality, and perhaps confidence. Here extensive re-training involving starting from scratch is probably not required; what will be necessary, though, will be to increase the amount of practice and coaching, with plenty of reassurance. Do not leave the person to stumble on.

For example, you may have passed your driving test with flying colours – several years ago. Could you pass that same test in an hour from now?

This isn't to suggest that you can't drive well, but passing the driving test probably requires brushing up on those procedures, skills and knowledge that are particular to the test. What is the stopping distance in the wet when driving at 60 mph, for instance?

If the person does the task regularly and has done the work correctly in the recent past, and their performance has deteriorated, the first thing to check out is whether it is still a Skills issue and whether their skills need recalibrating. What can happen is that bad skill habits can develop, or the person may not realise that their standards have slipped. Here the action is firstly to increase the amount of feedback, as a result of which the performance problem may become self-correcting. If this does not happen you will need to provide remedial training or coaching, and then, importantly, to monitor the results. This brings us to Box 8.

THE LIBERATOR

Box 8: Can't Do (Skills) issue – is the person still having problems?

If the person is still having problems, there is one further step to check out, providing that you are still sure that the problem is in the Can't Do rather than the Won't Do category. Hang on to your perseverance – some people are hares and others are tortoises – the tortoise can complete the same journey in the end and can then turn in a solidly consistent good performance. Equally, if you are developing someone to take on a new set of skills, you may have caused that person to struggle with a chunk of learning that is just too large for them to grasp.

Box 9: Can't Do (Skills) issue – is the job badly designed, or could it be simplified?

Sometimes a job is so poorly designed that the design itself affects good performance.

In one case, a production line team found that, after a work method readjustment, they were physically unable to carry out the required tasks, despite being skilled and experienced operators who had previously performed well.

Often the job can be simplified, or the piece of learning 'chunked down' into more digestible bites as a way of helping someone to perform the job well, enabling progress. It is important to check the job design before moving on to Box 10.

Box 10: Can't Do (Skills) issue – does the person have appropriate potential for this work?

The person has tried – it's not a case of Won't Do but Can't Do. You have done all you can to enable the person to succeed, have followed the steps, given time and attention, and acted with High Challenge-High Support.

It is crucial to maintain the perspective of High Challenge-High Support. You may feel sorry for the individual, but you will not be doing them, you, your team or the organisation any favours by carrying on. It will be debilitating for the individual and the team's overall performance.

People have different kinds of potential – not everyone can be a brain surgeon (not least because a number of us faint at the sight of blood!). Perhaps a more common example is that of selling, where, despite trying so hard to succeed it causes stress, some people find selling is not for them. The person is still OK and needs to be treated with Positive Regard. The particular kind of work is not suitable for them that is all; other kinds will suit them better. Redeploy the person to more suitable work, if possible. If not you will need to move towards severance while doing all you can to maintain that person's dignity and self-respect. They (and you) have tried. It's not a Won't Do but a Can't Do.

This may sound harsh, but not dealing with the situation is likely to prove harsher still in the long run.

We'll return now to the Won't Do part on the Performance Navigator, where the person is capable of doing what is required, but somehow doesn't do so consistently or can't be relied upon to do so. In these situations, people are operating to an agenda of their own as there will be a payoff for them of some kind – it may be some form of reward or may be to avoid negative outcomes or penalties. These can be subtle, as we will see, such as preferring to stay within the security of a comfort zone rather than experiencing the discomfort of moving outside it.

Box 11: Won't Do (Attitude) issue – does the person feel that it doesn't matter whether they perform well or not?

If the person feels that it doesn't matter, then this is the classic situation of Low Challenge-Low Support, resulting in apathy and low commitment. From the leader's point of view, it's also a classic example of 'you get what you give'.

People who are left in this position, despite perhaps their early good intentions, will find it increasingly difficult

M2: GET TO THE ROOT OF ISSUES

to maintain a good performance in such a void. This is particularly so when the norms of the group to which they belong are that 'it doesn't matter'. In this situation, without feedback and stimulation, what people do at work loses meaning and satisfaction, and they will find it increasingly difficult to invest themselves in it. Here there are no rewards, or recognition, if people do a good job. Neither are there penalties or comeback (another form of recognition) if they perform poorly – so why bother?

As we will see, recognition of what we do is so important for the great majority of people; without recognition, it is as though we don't exist. Classic 'jobsworth' behaviour – 'It's more than my job's worth' – the antithesis of empowerment, often results from the attitudes thus developed.

Here the message is to keep your nose clean, keep a low profile, don't inconvenience yourself, don't do anything that can go wrong, do just what the rules say – you won't be thanked for doing anything different and you won't get into trouble.

The crucial point is that it has to matter to the individual concerned, and this can be achieved through appropriate rewards and penalties. Take an individual, for example, who has to draft a report each month on behalf of the leader. The report is often of such poor quality, or late, that the leader ends up writing it, staying behind to do so and not addressing the performance issue with the staff member. It doesn't matter to the individual here whether they perform or not, the report may seem to them to be of little consequence. It is only when there are consequences to the individual that timelines and quality will be improved.

A common cause of leaders operating in a way which causes people to feel that it doesn't matter whether they perform well or not is because the leader has low expectations about what people are capable of achieving – 'you get what you give'. Sometimes, leaders operate in the 'doesn't matter' style because they can't be bothered, sometimes in the mistaken belief of confusing abdication for delegation/ empowerment, and sometimes because they lack the assertiveness or will to deal with the situation.

One practical example of what can happen is when a new leader is appointed to a team. In the early days, the team will test out the new leader, perhaps gently and subtly, perhaps more overtly. One of the members might, say, start finishing early. The other members will be watching – if that person 'gets away with it' then others will start to follow, if the person doesn't then the rest know where they stand.

The opposite of people feeling that their performance doesn't matter is, of course, when it does matter, and it is the approach and action of the leader which makes the difference. We are not being punitive here when we talk of rewards and penalties of High Challenge-High Support. Rather we would argue that although it may

M2: GET TO THE ROOT OF ISSUES

seem comfortable at one level, and an easy life, the 'doesn't matter' situation is not a healthy or enviable one. To be without recognition is to be impoverished.

Effective Leader-Developers have zero tolerance for 'doesn't matter' induced poor performance. Zero tolerance is part of the 'broken window' theory, increasingly being used as a demonstrably successful way to fight crime. The idea and philosophy is simple. If a broken window is not repaired, others are soon smashed, and before long the building is wrecked. The squalor encourages lawlessness and minor crime and, in due course, spawns more serious crime. If, on the other hand, the window is repaired, a positive environment is maintained and people are more likely to respect the law. It is all about dealing with problems in their infancy and not allowing them to escalate to become more major.

The feeling that it doesn't matter is, of course, the 'broken window' of *The Liberator* approach. Let us be clear that we are not linking poor performance at work with criminality, rather pointing out that the 'broken window' approach fits in the workplace too. The window is broken, in this sense if there is no recognition through rewards and penalties for good performance – it doesn't actually matter whether the person performs well or not. The approach in such cases is to find the right rewards and penalties, those which have a consequence to the person concerned, and to apply them consistently until they have a sustained effect.

Box 12: Won't Do (Attitude) issue – does the person feel penalised for doing the right thing?

A works manager placed much emphasis on wanting his managers to take initiative. When asked what happened when they did and got it right his reply was 'Nothing, it's their job'. When asked what happened when they used their initiative and got it wrong, he replied 'I tell them off' (or words to that effect). It transpired that his managers rarely, if ever, took the initiative – not surprisingly since they learned quickly that doing what was 'right' resulted never in reward, only in penalties.

When you have an inconvenient or unpleasant task to be done, who do you tend to give it to, the person who complains least or the one who complains most? If you consistently give such tasks to the person who complains least, then you are penalising that person for doing the 'right thing' of being co-operative and willing. Likewise, at home, which child receives the most attention, the one who creates the most fuss, or the one who is well behaved? And will the latter start to feel penalised for doing the right thing and change their behaviour to get some attention?

If the person does feel penalised for doing the right thing, then you must act to remove the penalties.

Box 13: Won't Do (Attitude) issue – are there good outcomes if the person does the wrong thing?

One obvious example is when an individual creates difficulties about taking on a task which then ends up elsewhere. A less obvious one perhaps, is where the reward comes from having a nickname or reputation for not performing – eg 'He's a real maverick'. Another is staying within the security of a comfort zone rather than experiencing the discomfort of moving outside it, even though it is in both the individual's and the organisation's interest to take on a wider range of work.

Which of your people gets the most attention from you, those who do the wrong thing or those who perform well? In mental institutions it was realised that patients who created the most disturbance got the most attention; it did not take long for other patients to realise that if they wanted attention they should act in the same way. Staff, too, learned that they needed to reward the good behaviour not just give attention to those doing the 'wrong' thing.

It is easy to inadvertently reward the wrong thing. One large company needed to reduce staff numbers; they were very well intentioned and the redundancy terms it offered were particularly generous. It had four times the number of volunteers it needed, which created a dilemma for the company. In the end, they only allowed the poor performers to go (who got rewarded for doing the wrong thing?). The good performers, of course, felt penalised for doing the right thing, and learned quickly that if they wanted to receive the same package next time round, they had better become poor performers. Absenteeism, lateness, quality and output deteriorated dramatically.

When the situation is one where there are good outcomes if the person does the wrong thing, then the leader must change that situation by creating positive outcomes for good performance, and include negative outcomes if the poor performance continues.

If the performance issue is a Won't Do one and you still haven't found the answer, there is one further possibility to consider.

Box 14: Won't Do (Attitude) issue – are there any job design characteristics which get in the way of good performance?

For example, a PA who is required to produce detailed, accurate typing of a manuscript and at the same time answer a constant stream of queries, despite having both high Can Do and Will Do, is unlikely to be able to get into the rhythm required.

Another example would be with air traffic controllers where the concentration required means that the job design, as well as the equipment and layout, has to be such to guarantee high performance.

There may be, in the situation, inappropriate equipment or poor job design which inhibit good performance. We are not talking about a perfect working environment here, but factors which are the root cause of poor performance, despite high Can Do and Will Do. These tend to happen rarely, but for both fairness and accurate diagnosis, they need to be considered.

The final question to be addressed, in the rare cases of a person who is still not performing to a satisfactory standard through lack of Will Do, is at Box 15.

Box 15: Won't Do (Attitude) issue – does the person have appropriate potential for this work?

If the leader has faced the situation squarely, using High Challenge-High Support, acting with appropriate Positive Regard and Genuineness, and having diagnosed the root cause of the performance issue accurately, has followed through with vigour and resolution, then, in a very few cases, the person may not have appropriate potential for the particular work. This can be so even when it is not a Skill issue, but a Will or attitude issue. It may be that the particular problem has become so entrenched (possibly because it was not addressed previously) or is so deep-rooted that it is beyond the time and capability of the leader to remedy.

In such a situation, High Challenge is again called for, where the leader has to accept the Challenge that, having genuinely done all that they can, it is time to resolve the situation and move on. In some circumstances, this may mean invoking the formal disciplinary procedures, or redeploying them to more suitable work, or even dismissal. This may be painful and involve difficulties, but the alternative of not dealing with the situation and bringing it to resolution is likely to be yet more painful in the long run.

It should only be the exceptional case which gets to this stage. The vast majority of performance issues are capable of being resolved, but only if the Leader-Developer is able to diagnose the root cause of the issue. They can then deal with the person, as a person, in the ways described in the following chapters.

The following case study illustrates this well, in addition to demonstrating how proper diagnosis is the starting point for resolving performance issues.

> **CASE STUDY: JILL**
>
> Jill Smith was the Accounts Controller for XYZ Ltd. Each month she had to collate data from some thirty or so line managers across a number of sites and include this data in a report for the Board.
>
> The performance issue was that the line managers, over whom Jill had no direct authority, were

M2: GET TO THE ROOT OF ISSUES

inconsistent in providing the data on time. It was a simple task for them, but they were busy people with many competing demands on their time, and often they did not give high priority to what Jill needed doing. This was creating a severe difficulty for Jill whose own report was often late, for which she was criticised. As well as this, she and her staff spent a great deal of time chasing up and giving reminders to line managers every month end, and also persuading them that the task was important, and reviewing the system to see whether it could be improved. Jill's staff were becoming demoralised, and Jill knew that the Board members were beginning to doubt her competence. On a personal level, she got on well generally with the line managers, and had sought their co-operation in getting their data in on time several times, but this only had a temporary effect.

What Jill did

Jill used the Performance Navigator to analyse the performance issue. She decided that it was the lack of performance on the part of the line managers which prevented her from performing and that the:

- Present Undesirable Behaviours were that line managers did not provide the data specified consistently and reliably, on time, or to the required accuracy
- Future Desirable Behaviours were for line managers to consistently and reliably, and without being reminded each month, provide the required data on time and to the required accuracy

Jill was also sure that they clearly knew what was expected, that they had the competence to do so, and that the problem was in the 'Won't Do' category. She decided, eventually, that the root cause of the issue landed in Box 11 of the Performance Navigator, in that the line managers felt that it didn't matter whether they performed or not.

She considered asking one of the directors whether to send the line managers a 'strong note', but rejected this idea as it made her appear and feel powerless, a victim in fact. Jill also realised that the effect of such a note would wear off over time and that she would be back to the old situation. She further rejected the idea of sending out reminders every month as the line managers were becoming dependent on this and, anyway, it was taking up too much of her time and that of her staff.

What Jill did was to send her report to the Board on time, even though she had to make estimates for the missing information, and to state in the report that it was incomplete because the necessary information had not been received from the line managers named. This created positive outcomes for those not named and negative outcomes for those named.

However, the most important and impressive part of what Jill did was not so much what she did, but how she did it. She hung on to her Positive Regard for the line managers who had caused her so much tribulation, and after agreeing her approach with her leader, she made a point of speaking to each line manager about the new system. She followed this up in writing, including the start date of the new approach, and deliberately did not resume the habit of reminding them.

The first month, of course, some line managers were still late and were 'named' in the way described. The reaction was interesting; those who were 'named' were embarrassed but felt it was a 'fair cop' – after all, they couldn't blame Jill, she had made a point of letting them know what was to happen, and the responsibility for not getting the data in was theirs. They felt OK about Jill and didn't see her setting up a win-lose situation.

If, however, Jill had sprung the new situation on them without warning, setting them up to fail in fact, the late line managers would still probably have felt it was a 'fair cop', but one that was unfair in that it was set up to be a win-lose instead of a win-win. The problem with a win-lose, of course, is that somehow or other it always gets turned into a lose-lose.

It would have been so easy for Jill to have resorted to 'war games' in the action she decided, particularly as the situation had given her some difficulties. Deciding the action, based on a good diagnosis, is not enough – it needs to be carried through with both High Challenge-High Support, and with Positive Regard and Genuineness.

In this particular situation, the data was consistently provided, on time, after the first month. The solution endured.

Chapter summary

M1: Be Explicit

The Liberator:

- Appreciates that Explicitness is a key skill, core to being an effective Leader-Developer.

- Understands the two elements of Explicitness are: the skill of defining in clear behavioural terms exactly what is required for good performance, and what will be regarded as poor performance – so the person has a clear mental picture of exactly what is required.

- Carries out correctly their use of Explicitness, with Positive Regard, so that it is helpful and not insulting or patronising – as it positions the person to succeed.

- Focuses on behaviour and not someone's personality or values as described in the Onion Model. Personality and values are not amenable to change and will be experienced anyway as a personal attack. Addressing behaviours, what someone actually does, is legitimate, focuses on what matters, is less threatening, and makes it easier to act upon.

- Uses the Change Sheet to help them think clearly about the performance issue; they then define

Present Undesirable Behaviours and Future Desirable Behaviours. Where there is a range of issues, they start with one or two, to build performance step-by-step.

M2: Get to the Root of Issues

The Liberator:

- Knows the first step in solving people's performance problems is to diagnose the problem accurately.

- Recognises that people aren't daft – they do things for a reason. They tend to do things they find rewarding and avoid doing things where there is a negative consequence or payoff for them.

- Understands that what gets rewarded gets done, you get more of the behaviours you reward, and it is so very easy to inadvertently reward the wrong thing.

- Works on the basis that people don't have to be ill to get better. In other words, the process applies to competent or good performers, who could do even better, as well as to currently poor performers.

- Makes effective use of the Performance Navigator to systematically identify the cause of

THE LIBERATOR

the issue, and associated rewards and penalties, separating issues into Can't Do (Skills) issues, and Won't Do (attitude) issues.

- Appreciates that most performance issues, once the person knows clearly what is expected, are 'Won't Do' ones. They decide a solution, act on it and follow up, then move on to the next issue.

THE SECRETS: MOBILISING STEP - UNCOVERED

M3: Be Appropriately Assertive
Build your own sense of assertion
Broken Record technique

M4: Give Empowering Feedback
Maximise people's performance through feedback
Powerful use of rewards and penalties as part of feedback
Rewards available to the Leader-Developer
Conditional and unconditional feedback
The flight plan analogy
Catch someone doing something right
Skills of giving positive feedback
Skills of giving negative feedback
Chapter summary

'Leadership is lifting a person's vision to higher sights, the raising of a person's performance to a higher standard, the building of a personality beyond its normal limitations.'
— Peter F Drucker

M3: Be Appropriately Assertive

> Apply appropriately the underlying skills and attitudes of assertiveness, which are necessary for being explicit and giving feedback, but also to maintain consistency of standards and approach; exert strong leadership when necessary to prevent the team going in different directions.

Build your own sense of assertion

Our experience is that having a clear sense of assertion is frequently one of the least-developed sets of characteristics and skills that is needed for developing high performance. It is, however, the influencing style which underpins the giving of feedback, especially negative feedback. It is also needed to support the High Challenge part of the High Challenge-High Support mindset, and for many it helps with Genuineness. There are other styles that the Leader-Developer needs to have in their repertoire, but assertion is the keystone of the set.

The culture of some environments seems to be almost entirely based on logical persuasion – a kind of debate to persuade, based on logic and the rationality of a point of view. In many performance issues this does not work very well, and degenerates into arguments and diversions, whereas an assertive-based approach is more likely to succeed. Then again, being Non-Assertive means that issues are not confronted and dealt with, leaving people in a void of not knowing where they stand, or praise is not given, at least not given well.

For some leaders, part of the difficulty is that they confuse assertion with aggression, or feel assertion is being too pushy. It isn't.

AGGRESSIVE	ASSERTIVE	NON-ASSERTIVE
Standing up for oneself and one's rights in a way that the rights of others are violated in the process	Standing up for oneself and one's rights in such a way that the other person's rights are not violated	Failing to stand up for oneself and one's rights effectively
The middle of the 'Onion' is attacked	Only the outer rings of **'Behaviour'** and **'Attitudes'** are addressed	
I Win - You Lose	I Win - You Win	You Win - I Lose

When leaders who are confused by this difference are encouraged to be strongly assertive, the recipient is usually surprised that the interaction was thought to be anywhere near aggression. In fact, what is most likely to happen with non-assertive leaders is that, at some stage, they flip from being non-assertive to aggressive when their 'doormat' bank is full. Clearly this, with its consequences, is something to avoid.

What is more advantageous is to build up the Personal Power of Assertion, so that there is plenty in reserve when difficult situations have to be dealt with. In some ways it is analogous to what often happens when people develop martial arts – confidence grows, and shows, so that the more capable someone is the less likely they are to have to use such skills, and when they do it is all well under control. A course delegate said to me:

> 'My definition of support would include respecting someone (sometimes oneself) enough to "tell the truth", if necessary. I find this kind of support more difficult; it's easier to cop out. But it feels much more authentic to be honest.
>
> 'One small but memorable example from my own past experience concerned a man who was about to join me, from another team, to work on a new project. I was aware that he came to work late, went home early and spent much of the time he was in completing *The Telegraph* crossword.
>
> 'After a lot of thought I knew it was only fair for me to be up front about what I expected as his

THE LIBERATOR

team leader. He was fifty-five and I was young enough to be his daughter, but, scared as I was, I confronted him.

'To my astonishment he said "No problem, no one has ever even noticed my timekeeping before. I won't let you down". And he didn't; he worked hard and was much happier for it. A valuable lesson for us both I believe.'

Another way of looking at assertion is back to the OK Corral:

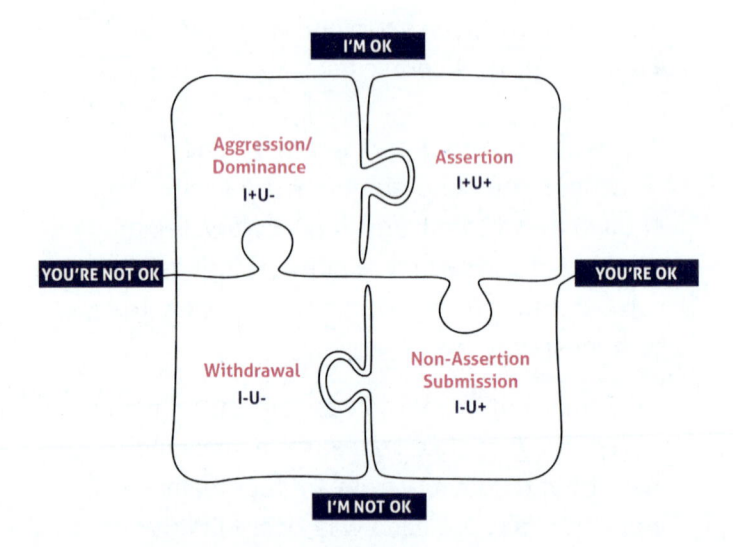

```
                    I'M OK
         ┌──────────────┬──────────────┐
         │ Aggression/  │              │
         │ Dominance    │  Assertion   │
         │    I+U-      │    I+U+      │
YOU'RE   │              │              │ YOU'RE
NOT OK   ├──────────────┼──────────────┤   OK
         │              │ Non-Assertion│
         │  Withdrawal  │  Submission  │
         │    I-U-      │    I-U+      │
         └──────────────┴──────────────┘
                  I'M NOT OK
```

Assertion is based on the I+U+ position, a dialogue between two mature adults as it were, both capable of accepting responsibility for their actions, both OK people with rights which need to be respected. One of the rights of the other person is to be treated as

M3: BE APPROPRIATELY ASSERTIVE

fundamentally OK (personality and values), even though their behaviour or attitude may not have been OK on this occasion.

Again, another of these rights is to be praised and recognised for what has been achieved when it is real and significant (U+), rather than patronised or manipulated from a U- one (disguised or transparent). The rights of the leader include the absolute requirement to develop high performance in the team and to tell people when they are not delivering.

Staying in the I+U+ position is desperately important when giving feedback; it's an all-purpose ground rule which is the key to handling all kinds of situations, including difficult and contentious ones.

The essence of Assertion is expressed in the following two figures.

Assertiveness Mindset

Stay in the I+U+ position	If this is difficult, hang on to your Positive Regard and don't get 'hooked' into aggression, allowing yourself to be aggressed upon or dealing with the other person like a child. If you stay in the I+U+ position, the probability is that the other person will eventually respond in the same way.
Look after your rights, and the rights of the other person	You have legitimate rights, such as being respected as an individual, being treated with courtesy, having a point of view, asking for what you want, to be human and make a mistake, being listened to - so does the other person. Don't trample the other person's rights.

Assertiveness Skills and Behaviours

Use the 'I' statement	Not 'one', 'we', 'they', 'the company', 'my boss', 'the organisation', 'the rules' - but 'I'. Hiding behind other people dilutes the power of its message; this is from you. Remember the greatest reward you have to give is yourself. What is said has to come from you directly and you have to own it, whether it is praise or reprimand.
Keep it short and succinct - cut the waffle	Be direct and clear in saying what you want and need. Come to the point quickly and don't confuse the other person with a mass of verbiage or camouflage - just say what is on your mind and don't dress it up.
Avoid qualifiers	Qualifiers like 'perhaps', 'maybe', 'a little', 'if you wouldn't mind', etc, fog and weaken the message, and get in the way. Again keep it short and succinct.
Express your feelings	'I feel angry that', 'I feel pleased that', 'I feel desperate that', 'I feel worried that', 'I feel delighted that'. The power of the praise or reprimand comes from you; if it is authentic then feelings will show. This is not to say that you should lose your temper, shout or kiss the other person, but do let them know how you feel about what has happened. In this we differ from many other writers on Assertion, where feelings do not enter the equation. Assertion without humanity can be experienced as an impersonal routine and result in a resistance of its own making.
Avoid irritators	Sarcasm or stings/tweaks like 'I want you to do this... if you are capable of doing it', leak from a fundamentally I+U- position. Keep the Assertion clean and uncontaminated.
Use appropriate body language	Look at the other person, be there, relax, use an even tone of voice and, on occasions, count to ten and take a deep breath. Stay in I+U+ position.

Assertiveness is what underpins the giving of effective feedback. This is perhaps more obvious with the giving of negative feedback, but it is necessary, too, when giving positive feedback. The experience of participants on training programmes shows that, when they are asked to give some praise to someone else, what frequently happens is that the praiser does not look at the person being praised, a joke is made of it to cover embarrassment, or the praise has a 'put down' quality and does not address a real issue. Many of us are not very good at giving praise. Yet, when a genuine piece of praise is well given, the effect on the person receiving it is striking.

A concern that people who are reluctant to use assertion often have is that they feel they might be discourteous (as well as being experienced as aggressive, as referred to earlier). To lay things out clearly and simply is not being discourteous (in our UK culture at least), it is clarifying, helpful and respectful.

Broken Record technique

One final assertion technique which Leader-Developers find useful when dealing with people who are adept at avoiding personal responsibility for what has happened, fudging issues or deflecting away from the point, is called the 'Broken Record'.

This simply involves sticking to the point you are making and not allowing yourself to be deflected, doing so by repeating what you want until the message is heard (hence the name Broken Record). An example of this would be:

> Leader: 'In future, I want you to write down what actions we agree that you should take following our weekly meetings.'
>
> Team Member: 'I don't need to write them down, I can remember.'
>
> Leader: 'I understand that, but I want you to write them down so they don't get missed.'
>
> Team Member: 'Why do I have to do it when no one else is?'
>
> Leader: 'We are not discussing anyone else now, I want you to write down the agreed actions.'
>
> Team Member: 'What difference will it make?'
>
> Leader: 'I want you to write them down so you don't forget them.'
>
> Team Member: 'OK.'

Note how the leader kept repeating what they required and did not allow things to be side-tracked down other avenues. Avoiding being rude, and not allowing the team member to evade the issue, gave extra strength to the point being made.

The Broken Record technique is very difficult to resist and, again, staying in the I+U+ mode is crucial.

M4: Give Empowering Feedback

> Deliver feedback, both positive and negative, clearly and continuously, to reinforce positive results and correct the negative ones, in order to help the person to improve rapidly.

Maximise people's performance through feedback

Feedback allows people to know whether they are on course or not, where they are, how they are doing. It is a crucial part of the navigation system for continuous improvement. The feedback is only useful if it is explicit, relevant, focuses on behaviour and, above all, is heard. It also needs to be delivered step-by-step, little and often.

In the context of developing performance, feedback is given for the purpose of encouraging someone to do more (or less) of the same. When reinforced with the right rewards or consequences it guides and shapes efficient performance, and encourages growth, personal mastery and success – which we will delve further into in a moment. This is so whether correcting present poor performance, helping someone through the

Transition Curve of change, coaching someone from Dependency to Interdependence, or conducting an enabling appraisal. Feedback provides personal security, reassurance and certainty in an often otherwise turbulent and confusing world. It allows people to know:

- Where they stand
- What is expected of them
- How they are performing
- How they are progressing

A consequence of the feedback is that it makes it easier for people to take increasing responsibility for developing themselves and becoming the best they can be.

An example of the power of simple, explicit and continual feedback is shown in this short real-life situation:

> A consultant had to make a presentation to a group he did not know, in a venue deep in the heart of some countryside with which he was unfamiliar. There was very little space in his schedule to get there on time. Despite his experience in giving such presentations, he felt a degree of anxiety; the presentation was important for his partners and himself and the journey would be long and arduous.
>
> The directions to find the venue provided by the hotel were excellent. It said things like, 'You

> will see a large station on your right, the sign to XYZ you are looking for is a few hundred yards past this on the left', and 'once you have gone past the Mucky Duck pub on your left, start looking for a fork, and take the right fork'.

The point of the story is that the directions provided continual feedback so that the driver, in unfamiliar territory and doing something new, knew how he was doing and that he was on track in his search for the conference venue. They allowed him to get to his destination efficiently and on time. Importantly, they had the effect of removing from the situation the anxiety and stress that otherwise would have been present.

In this case, the directions, their Explicitness, and the feedback that was an integral part of them, were enabling for the consultant as they helped him perform at his best.

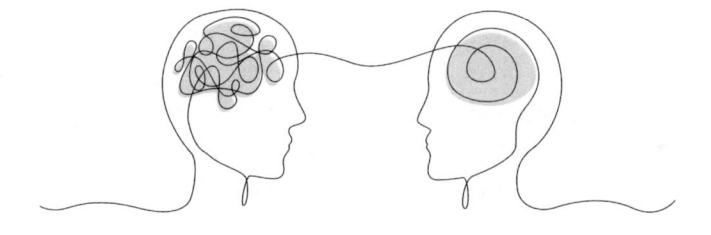

Picking up on the point about reinforcing the approach through the use of the right rewards and penalties, effective Leader-Developers have honed this skill well. They know this helps them to maximise performance through feedback, and build engagement and motivation in their people, in their quest to resolutely move them to the Developing Step, which we cover in Chapter 5.

Right here, right now, at the Mobilising Step, we need to spend time looking at this secret because it evades so many leaders and because it is such an integral part of giving feedback. It is the effective use and rewards and penalties.

Powerful use of rewards and penalties as part of feedback

> Legend has it that in the early days of a now-major electronics company, one of the founders was in his office working late when, without pausing to knock, in burst a research scientist shouting, 'I've done it, I've done it!'
>
> The founder knew the importance of the project the scientist was working on and the effort that had gone into it. It was a moment of celebration; spontaneously, he wanted to give the scientist something to show his appreciation and mark the moment. Pulling open his desk drawer all he could find was a banana. Speechlessly – because he could not find the right words to say, so great was the significance of the achievement to the fledgling company – he held out the banana for the scientist to take, both parties recognising immediately what it meant.

> The company now has the 'Golden Banana Award', where a small golden banana marks and celebrates occasions of high achievement.

People tend to do more of the things they find rewarding, and what they find unrewarding, they tend to do less of. The Leader-Developer can have much influence on both aspects of this, remembering the old adage, 'What gets rewarded gets done!'

Rewards, and penalties, shape behaviour and habits and cause people to perform well or not, to develop and grow. They are tangible expressions of whether people are 'on course' or not, they let people know where they stand and how they are doing, and they provide the context in which effort will be applied or withheld. In a Low Challenge-Low Support environment, for example, apathy and alienation will reign, while in a High Challenge-High Support context there will be commitment and endeavour.

Without appropriate rewards, particularly those where feedback is involved, people are working in a void; they are being asked to roller skate in the dark on the top of a tall building, to use the analogy that was introduced in Chapter 1.

It is also easy, inadvertently or otherwise, to reward the wrong thing, as was seen in Chapter 3. Organisations may, for example, proclaim the importance they place on team working, but if the appraisal system and other reward mechanisms do not reflect this, and focus on individual achievement only, then collaboration will not occur – internal competition will.

We are not talking here of Pavlovian dogs or what Hertzberg called 'Jumping for the Jelly Beans'. Rather the emphasis and intent is to facilitate and enable people to be successful in developing their abilities, performance and potential; or to grow perhaps from Dependency to Interdependence; or to be able to 'surf the waves of change' rather than being swamped by them. Giving appropriate rewards is not only a Transactional process based on improving day-to-day performance, but also a leadership-based Transformational one, aimed at achieving the vision of a person performing at their very best and achieving their full potential. The underlying ethos is to enable rather than to control.

Of course, individuals will differ in their levels of motivation and the types of motivation patterns, and in their experience and maturity in a job, which in turn will affect the kind of rewards that are most suitable. It's a case of 'different strokes for different folks'. Motivation and Leadership Styles will be explained subsequently as an important way of fine-tuning the approach.

Rewards available to the Leader-Developer

If a group of managers were to brainstorm a list of rewards which were available to them to award, and how each reward might be applied, the results might look like those in the following table... along with coffee, cake and doughnuts!

Money	This is only effective if there is a strong and demonstrable link between performance and rewards.
Promotion	Leaders usually cannot offer a firm promise of promotion but they can help their people to perform well and highly to improve their chances, and champion their cause.
Security	Security comes from being employable and flexible, that is performing capably and being able to cope with change.
Recognition	Praise, increased responsibility, trust, 'well done', letters of congratulation, freedom and many more are all forms of recognition, as are the symbolic ones of giving cakes, coffee, bananas etc.
Time Off	Accommodating requests from good performers (but not poor ones) or 'job and finish' are examples of rewards.
Fun	Making work zestful, developing team spirit, celebrating achievements, competitions - creating enjoyment so that people want to pull out the stops and show what they can do.
Learning and Personal Growth	Being challenged, learning new skills, developing experience.
Interesting or Favourite Work	Allocation of such work to high performers as a reward.
Ownership, Responsibility and Delegation	Trusting good performers by making the job 'theirs'.
Job Satisfaction	By creating meaning to the work and developing personal mastery to do it well.
Self-Esteem and Worth	Through creating and reinforcing actual competence and contribution.

The difference between extrinsic and intrinsic rewards

When such a typical list is examined more closely, it is apparent that some of the rewards are extrinsic, that is, provided by an 'outside' stimulus, such as money, a larger office or a new car. Others are intrinsic – psychological rewards experienced directly by the individual. So, some rewards come from the outside, while others harmonise with what is already important for the person; they connect with what is there. It is the intrinsic rewards which can have the greatest and most long-term effect.

This is not to discount the importance of money and other extrinsic factors. The level of material reward has to be right, though, otherwise the relationship won't be seen as fair. However, there are a number of disadvantages to relying on material rewards only, especially money. It can become like Dane gold, where, in the days of the Vikings, the English kings bribed the Danes not to trouble them. It worked, but the problem was the price went up year by year until the Treasury was exhausted, and then the Danes invaded anyway. Relying on material rewards is a one-way losing bet, in the sense that all behaviour ends up having a price.

There is another compelling reason why reliance cannot be placed solely on material rewards. This is because they lie in the province of the organisation, not the individual leader. Salary scales, promotion systems, pension schemes and car policies are controlled by the organisation; a team member has access to them by virtue of being a member of the organisation. To put it crudely, once a team member is in the organisation, the same benefits will broadly apply to all the members of the team except, exceptionally, where extremely low performance carries the risk of a penalty, discipline or even termination, and exceptionally high performance gives the possibility of increased reward. For the majority though, broadly speaking, the same extrinsic rewards will apply to everyone.

Of course, the leader may be able to influence promotions, bonuses (if they apply) and performance-related pay where it is used. What is important, in performance-related pay, is that it is not the amount of differential award (often quite small, relative to the whole) which creates the effect, but the recognition involved. The leader also has an influence on material rewards in an arguably more important and less obvious way. That is, to help team members guarantee their security through the security of employability, which in turn requires the habits of high performance, flexibility and the ability to learn and cope with change.

A uni-dimensional reliance, by the leader, on material rewards is not a good idea, providing the level of such rewards is reasonable in the first place. If the rewards available to the leader to give are allocated across a scale, typically that scale would look something like this:

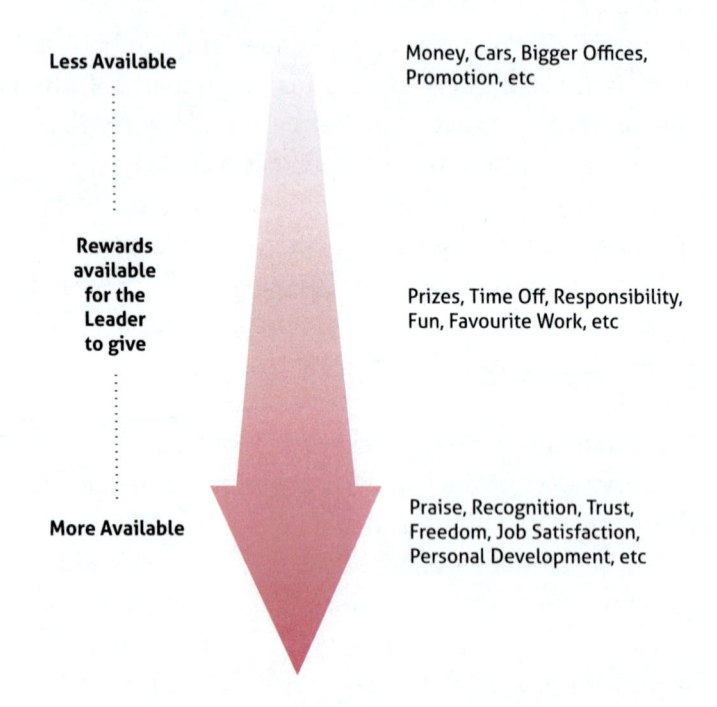

Less Available

Money, Cars, Bigger Offices, Promotion, etc

Rewards available for the Leader to give

Prizes, Time Off, Responsibility, Fun, Favourite Work, etc

More Available

Praise, Recognition, Trust, Freedom, Job Satisfaction, Personal Development, etc

The reward of recognition, given Genuinely

The set of rewards most available to effective leaders, and the ones effective Leader-Developers use most, are those such as praise, recognition, responsibility, trust, etc. There is a fortunate coincidence and paradox here: not only are such rewards – and penalties through the withholding of them – the most available to the leader, but they are also the most powerful. Study after research study has demonstrated that recognition consistently appears at the top, or close to the top, of people's requirements from work.

Praise, responsibility, trust and many other rewards are, essentially, to do with recognition. But – and it's an important but – that recognition has to be genuine and authentic, and underpinned by The Mindset of High Challenge-High Support, where there is both strong commitment to the person and a preparedness to give not just praise when due, but also to face and deal with inappropriate performance.

Many leaders seem to erect a glass screen between themselves and their team, and use 'management speak' which blurs the message and the relationship. What they say has little impact or meaning because it's not coming from them as a person, but from them in their role of leader. Equally, some leaders try to get so friendly with their team that they lose the ability to reprimand, a mistake often made by newly appointed leaders, especially when assigned to lead a team in which they were previously a member.

Remember: the greatest reward you have to give is yourself.

When you see something exceptional, when you see one of your people take an important step forward, when you see extra effort applied to overcome a problem, you will be delighted and you will say so. Nelson Mandela tells in his biography how, after many years in prison and when his spirits were at their lowest ebb, an unseen voice from a new guard said through the cell grille, 'I see you, Nelson Mandela, I respect you', and the powerful restorative impact that statement had on him.

The opposite also applies. When the task is done in a slipshod manner, when customers don't get the attention they deserve, and when problems are hidden or disguised, it will matter to you and you will express your disappointment, clearly and directly.

The psychological need for 'Stroking'

Why is it that recognition is such an important need for the majority of us?

In the language of Transactional Analysis (a psychological model which describes what happens between people, and why we often behave the way we do), such recognition is called 'Strokes', or 'Stroking'. People need Strokes to maintain their physical and psychological well-being.

For example, it is well established that babies and infants need physical contact (Stroking) of a positive, nurturing nature, to emotionally grow and prosper. There is evidence too, and more surprisingly, that a lack of such Stroking impairs the physical growth and well-being of the child.

M4: GIVE EMPOWERING FEEDBACK

As people move from childhood to adulthood, their need for Strokes continues, as does the need for recognition. The strength of this need is such that some people, in the absence of positive recognition, will contrive to seek 'put downs' and Negative Strokes, which are at least a form of recognition, and which are better than not being recognised at all.

What happens in our society is that, at a certain stage in adulthood, it becomes culturally unacceptable to Stroke people physically, such as by caressing them or with other physical contact – or indeed to be Stroked by them (except in the closest of relationships). Instead, we begin to use other forms of recognition, such as words, smiles, gestures, frowns, nods, etc.

A Positive Stroke is one which carries a 'You're OK' message and usually results in the recipient feeling good and reaffirmed. A Negative Stroke results in unpleasant feelings. How Strokes are given or received tends to reflect the life position in the OK Corral (shown in Chapter 1) that a person is in. People who feel OK about themselves and others tend to seek out exchanges of Positive Strokes; those who feel others are not OK tend to give Negative Strokes, and those who feel 'I'm not OK' tend to seek out Negative Strokes which will increase their 'not OK' feelings. The rule seems to be that Negative Strokes are better than no Strokes at all, although it is the Positive Strokes which nourish us.

Such is the power of recognition that some people have learned, through their life experiences, that they would rather be recognised through Negative Strokes than be ignored, and will choose to play the psychological game of 'kick me', where they set themselves up to be punished. This does, at least, result in some form of acknowledgement.

Conditional and unconditional feedback

Strokes, or feedback, may be conditional (for doing) or unconditional (for being) as follows:

Positive	UNCONDITIONAL	eg:	'I like you, you're a good bloke'
	CONDITIONAL	eg:	'That was a good report you produced; it was clear, concise and summed up the issues'
Negative	CONDITIONAL	eg:	'When someone has an idea you always criticise it right away, so people are reluctant to make suggestions. Next time someone has one, find something positive to say about it first, before pointing out the flaws'
	UNCONDITIONAL	eg:	'You're a waste of space'

Generally, positive unconditional feedback is more suited to the home or social life than to the workplace, while negative unconditional feedback has limited or no value anywhere. If we look at conditional and unconditional feedback as forms of recognition in terms of the Onion Model, we can see that negative unconditional

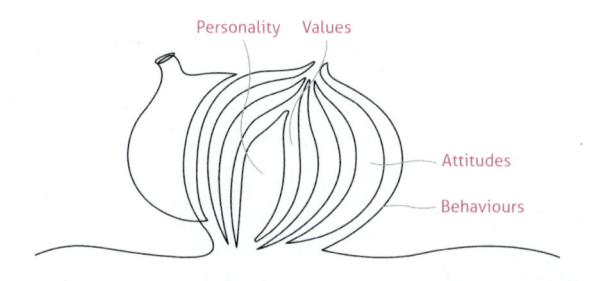

Diagram: an onion with layers labeled Personality, Values, Attitudes, Behaviours.

feedback will be experienced as attacking the core integral self and will provoke the kind of reaction they deserve. Unconditional positive feedback, although nourishing, does not change workplace behaviour. Conditional feedback though, influences behaviour and, importantly, attitudes – for example, through praise and recognition when good performance is achieved, and through negative feedback when it is not.

Once again, what is critically important in all this is the underlying mindset of 'I'm OK, You're OK'. There is all the difference in the world in seeing the other person as basically OK, that is, having fundamental worth and value, and with Positive Regard, even though what they may have done on a given occasion (their behaviour) was not appropriate. It is not the person who is not OK, but their behaviour.

It is when this mindset is present that negative conditional feedback (or a reprimand) will be received and most usually accepted. Without The Mindset, the recipient will resist or resent being viewed this way, and also feel aggrieved if the negative feedback was unconditional. Further, if you stay in the I'm OK, You're

OK mindset, even if you yourself are feeling aggrieved, or when the other person is operating from an I'm not OK, You're not OK stance, then the chances are that, in both cases, they will eventually shift to an I'm OK, You're OK dialogue with you.

The importance of consistency

What also matters is the crucial leadership characteristic of consistency. You can't start giving feedback then stop. To be seen as an authentic *Liberator* of people, giving empowering feedback and using the full range of rewards and penalties available will be what helps people to improve rapidly. The recognition and praise you give them through this process help them to shine.

Generalised praise, particularly when it is not genuine but a ritual, is not helpful and can be patronising. Praise and thanks as part of everyday courtesy is something else again. But what we are talking about here is recognition for a specific action or piece of behaviour to encourage more of the same, which is much more than an everyday courtesy. Such recognition can be verbal or nonverbal, or, as in the banana story, symbolic or tangible. It marks and celebrates what has been achieved by way of a step forward.

We are not just talking about major achievements here, but any significant move in the direction you want the

M4: GIVE EMPOWERING FEEDBACK

person to take. Change is a series of small steps, each one reinforced on a little-and-often basis. Equally, as well as rewards, the use of consequences or penalties reinforces this process. It is for the Leader-Developer to be clear on the penalties available to them, which have to be thought about and enforced when the need arises. However, all the evidence is that rewards work better than penalties, and positive reinforcement through recognition has the greatest effect.

The cardinal rule is: catch someone doing something right!

This stands in opposition to the more usual: ignoring what is going well and 'blitzing' what is going wrong!

People aren't daft, they do things for a reason, and those reasons are the awards they obtain or the consequences they avoid. It is the doing of things, behaviour, which Leader-Developers concentrate on, so the right things get done. When the right things get done, consistently, attitudes are also likely to shift, which in turn consolidates and underpins the behaviour.

One final point here, just as giving your attention through feedback and recognition is the greatest reward you can give, removing your attention is the greatest penalty.

THE LIBERATOR

The flight plan analogy

Giving feedback is a 'moment of truth', the communication process through which the Leader-Developer, having diagnosed a performance issue, having decided in explicit terms what behaviours are and are not required, and having thought about appropriate rewards and consequences, puts it all into action.

This action is rather analogous to flying. For instance, if you turn up at Heathrow expecting to be flown to Acapulco, you will have a quite reasonable expectation that the pilot will land at the right airfield, will have enough fuel and will generally get you there safely. You expect the plane to be flown by a competent professional, able to deal appropriately with any incident or deviation en route. In particular, you will expect the pilot to know where they are, all the time, so that if the plane is off course, this can be corrected, and the plane brought back on track. Equally, it is rare that the course will be a completely straight one, both because of navigational hazards and other difficulties.

What pilots do, of course, is follow a flight plan. They don't expect to take off from Heathrow and worry about how they are going to get to their destinations later hopefully. So it is with effective Leader-Developers who deliver high performance.

These days aircrews can locate their position through global positioning electronic systems which give them constant feedback that they are on course. In fact, an alarm will activate if they are not. They are still required to fly over position beacons occasionally, which give an alternative, yet more certain position of where they are.

In the 'flight plan' of the Leader-Developer, their beacons are appraisal meetings, often formal. But one absolute difference between effective leaders and less effective ones is that the effective ones do not wait and store up feedback for regular appraisal reviews (the beacons) perhaps once or twice a year, instead they give instant feedback continuously, hour by hour where necessary, day by day, week by week. If they catch someone doing something right they say so, at the time, immediately; if a mistake is being made, or poor performance is observed, they deal with it there and then, rather than waiting for it to become a habit.

They are always on the lookout for good performance continuously, and catch and reinforce it immediately, for they know that positive reinforcement is much more effective than criticism.

Key

- Beacons in the form of regular management reviews allow feedback and re-routing as necessary
- GPS beeps in the form of regular praise and recognition confirm you are on track
- Reprimands (GPS alarm) pull you back on course

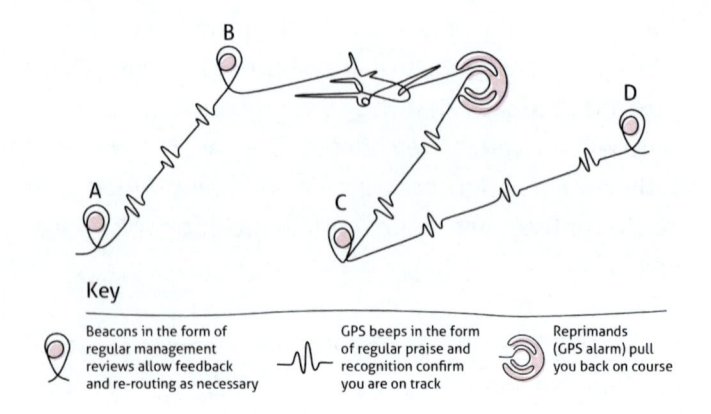

Catch someone doing something right

We need to define what we mean by 'catch someone doing something right'. What we mean is an improvement, a step in the right direction, something different. Of course, someone who performs reliably and consistently deserves thanks and appreciation. But to concentrate on giving praise for basic things, like attendance at team meetings, debases the currency of feedback.

Maintaining someone's already high performance requires, and deserves, appropriate and authentic recognition, beyond the normal courtesies. However, an improvement, a step in the right direction, is something else. It requires to be caught, celebrated and positively reinforced. This is what is meant by the phrase catch someone doing something right. You then encourage the next step and catch that being done right also.

It doesn't matter how small these steps are. Initially, they are likely to be quite small as in the case when someone is caught up in the log jam of established habits and practices. When they reach a landing, so to speak, between the steps, then that is the time to consolidate the achievement with additional praise and recognition. Beware though of repeatedly praising the completion of an individual step, because the message then becomes one of reinforcing the person to stay where they are, and not to move on to the next stage. It is a continuous journey, for true excellence is an always-moving state.

THE PIGEON ANALOGY

In the field of research, animals are often trained to perform certain tasks.

For example, pigeons have been trained to ring a bell. It was more than a million-to-one chance that they would succeed in ringing the bell without assistance.

The first step in their training was to get them to move towards the bell. When they did move a step towards it, they were rewarded with a grain of corn. If they had been stuffed full of corn at this stage, they would have stayed where they were and roosted, after all, the reward is of a scale that will reinforce this behaviour.

It was a further step, then a further, each of which got rewarded with small grains, that enticed them onwards, and when the bell was rung, the reward was special and treated as such.

We are not suggesting here that people are in any way like pigeons. But the example of a series of small, attainable steps towards a goal, each one reinforced with feedback and recognition (not in the form of corn!) is apt, particularly during the Transactional stage of Mobilising. When people are equipped with the basic skills and, more importantly, have developed the will to move further, then a different type of learning applies, which we move onto in Chapter 5.

At this Mobilising Step, Leader-Developers then provide feedback regularly and catch someone doing something right. While they also let people know when things are not going right, they are particularly on the lookout for the former. They have high expectations about their people's performance, have a vision (flight plan) about people performing at their very best, and are consistent. Their people know where they stand in that, if they do good work, it will be noticed and dealt with. Feedback becomes a way of life, people know in advance what to expect. In fact, the leader will describe to new members of the team how they will be receiving strong feedback regularly in order to help them, which goes right back to the Rights and Responsibilities of leaders and team members highlighted in Chapter 1. In this way, while negative feedback is given, it won't be experienced as though it were a jet fighter screaming out of the sun. People will know the rules of engagement; positive and negative feedback given where due. So, on these occasions when negative feedback is appropriate, it will be heard and responded to more.

We are back to The Mindset. The leader who develops high performance is not only skilled at giving feedback, it matters to them that the other person succeeds, and cares enough to give such feedback clearly and directly, both positive and negative.

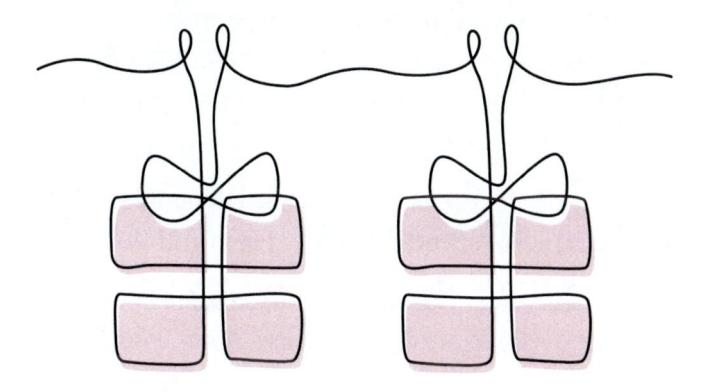

Skills of giving positive feedback

We can now move on to the skills of giving feedback, in a way that:

- Is assertively powerful and natural
- Focuses on behaviour (and not personality or values)
- Is part and parcel of everyday working life
- Takes a short time to do
- Helps people to improve and develop, and be recognised and rewarded.

Here are some simple tips for giving positive feedback through praise and recognition:

- Let people know, in advance, that you will be giving plenty of feedback
- Catch improved performance immediately – ten seconds of immediate praise will reinforce the action much more effectively than a comment a week later at a formal review meeting
- Describe the good performance explicitly and its consequences, and directly express your feelings
- Pause to allow the good feelings to sink in – the pause will also show them there is no 'sting in the tail'
- Encourage them to do more of the same

Sometimes, when praise is used for the first time or people have had a different experience of it in the past when it was not always used genuinely, they sometimes don't always 'hear' it. Should this happen, then it is useful to understand the reasons, so it can be better dealt with.

Why people sometimes don't hear praise

Waiting for the 'YES BUT': Many of us have been conditioned to view being 'patted' as a prelude to being 'kicked', or have impending criticism introduced by some praise to sweeten the pill:

- Keep the praise clear and uncontaminated
- Repeat the praise if necessary
- Make it clear when you want to deal with criticism and keep it separate

Embarrassment: Sometimes, people get embarrassed by praise, especially when they are not used to receiving it. Typically, they may want to move the subject on quickly:

- Wait out any embarrassed pauses, don't rush on, and let the praise sink in
- Repeat the praise later to give them a further chance to absorb it and accept it

It's not real: Occasionally, people have experienced praise just as a way of buttering them up or making them pliable. It is then experienced as not real or manipulative:

- Act out of Genuineness only
- Be specific about what the particular praise is for, make it conditional

Minimising it as unimportant: Occasionally someone might not see that a particular skill or action is important; they may take it for granted, overlooking its significance. Positive reinforcement though will encourage people to do more of the same thing and appreciate and value what they can contribute:

- Reinforce the praise
- Put it into context and explain why it is so important

Seeing it as a technique: Basically, here the praise is not seen as being genuine, but artificial; something perhaps that has been introduced on the latest course:

- Be Genuine with the praise you give
- Be consistent about giving it, but only when it is deserved

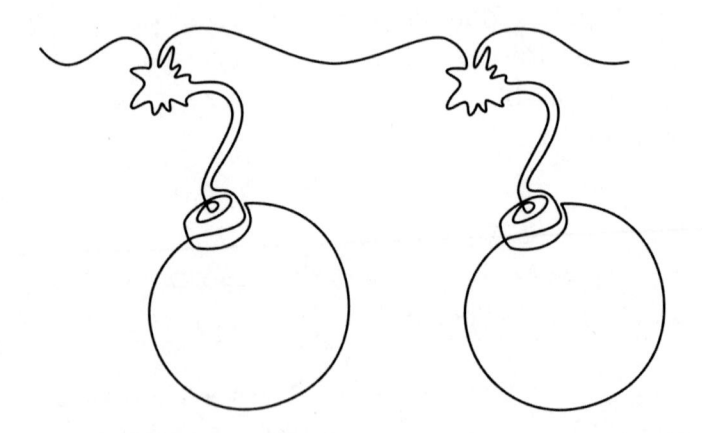

Skills of giving negative feedback

Negative feedback is the other side of the equation which makes the whole. Although it is positive feedback which tends to reinforce high performance the most, there will be occasions when negative feedback is necessary in the interests of the person, and to give a 'rounded' picture. Also, if people know that they will receive praise when due, this legitimises and makes acceptable the giving of negative feedback, and also makes the praise given to be experienced as valued and authentic.

There are two types of negative feedback:

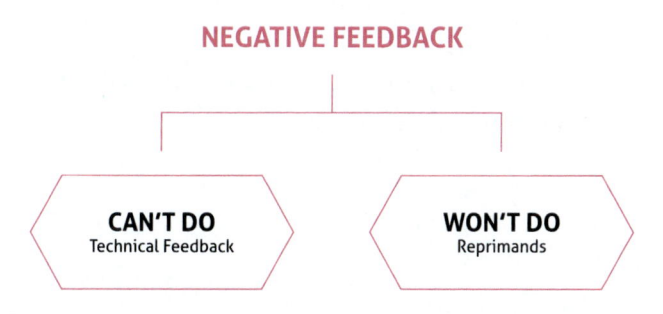

NEGATIVE FEEDBACK

- **CAN'T DO** — Technical Feedback
- **WON'T DO** — Reprimands

The first of these is where something has gone wrong, because of Can't Do; that is the team member didn't have the skills or knowledge to do what was required. The basic approach here is for the leader to accept that this was their responsibility, and to deal with the situation neutrally as a piece of learning. Then again, people will sometimes make the wrong judgements or decisions, not out of any lack of Will Do, but because their Can Do is not yet fully developed. This also needs to be dealt with as a learning opportunity.

If the person has the skills and knowledge required, then it will be a Won't Do situation, where a reprimand is more appropriate. The way to deal with a reprimand is to:

- Let people know, in advance, that you will be giving plenty of feedback

- Deal with poor performance immediately (but not in front of others)

- Stay in the I+U+ position, remember it is not the person but their behaviour that is the issue

- Describe explicitly the nature of the poor performance, its consequences and how you feel about it

- Pause for a second or two to allow the reprimand to sink in, look at the other person, let them feel your disappointment or displeasure

- Tell them what you require, and the consequences that will result

- Let them know you value them, but not their behaviour on this occasion
- Move on to something else, the reprimand is now over, it's done

Again, it is useful to understand why people sometimes don't 'hear' reprimands, and how to deal with negative reactions.

Why people sometimes don't hear reprimands

Shock: 'No one has ever told me that before.' Such news can confront someone's self-image in a disturbing way:

- Give time and space for the message to settle
- Reinforce they are OK as a person (but not that particular behaviour)

Denial: 'That's not right/true/accurate/fair', or whatever. Here the person just plain refuses to consider the feedback as part of a defence mechanism:

- Give specific behavioural examples to illustrate your point
- Stay calm but persistent and assertive, refusing to be drawn into an argument
- Seek agreement for them to think about what has been said

It's not fair: The 'It just came off in my hand, Mum' response or 'I'm better than many others, why pick on me?' approach. Here people are seeking to avoid responsibility for hearing the message by attempting to direct attention from themselves to elsewhere:

- Refuse to discuss other people
- Don't be diverted from the point, but be prepared to listen

Fear of being labelled/pigeonholed: 'This will be recorded somewhere', 'I'll be seen this way forever.' The resistance has to do with the fear of being labelled as 'blemished':

- Take a future orientation
- Remind them of their strengths, so the perspective is that of the whole picture

Anger at not being allowed to express their point of view: 'He's not listening to me so why should I bother listening to him? I'll switch off':

- Listen
- Demonstrate that you are listening by summarising, reflecting back, etc

M4: GIVE EMPOWERING FEEDBACK

- If necessary, ask questions to draw the other person out

Disagreement	Explain your view and listen actively to theirs; ask if they accept your view; agree to monitor the behaviour if necessary
Challenging	Defuse aggression; lower your voice; stick to questions only for a time; say something positive about the person
Hurt Silence	Allow emotional expression, ask 'How do you feel about that?' Show that you care and that it is OK to be emotional. 'That's OK, it's how you feel, tell me about it'. Repeat strong praise and turn the conversation to the future
Taking My Ball Home	Tackle the issue directly. 'I can see you have taken that to heart', and ask questions to push the person into Challenging (see above)
Dependency	DON'T do all the work for them. Ask them, 'What would you do to improve?' and don't be afraid of silences; wait for answers; push them into taking an active role

'Never look down on anybody unless you're helping him up.'
– Jesse Jackson

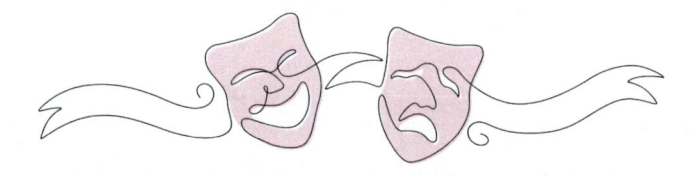

Chapter summary

M3: Be Appropriately Assertive

The Liberator:

- Builds their own sense of assertion to achieve win-win outcomes, and appreciates the power of assertion over aggression or non-assertion

- Understands the assertiveness mindset is to stay in the I+U+ position and employs the full range of assertiveness skills, which includes eye contact, getting to the point and expressing feelings to assist development

- Purposefully lean into their Personal Power to ensure they maintain the appropriate level of Assertiveness

M4: Give Empowering Feedback

The Liberator:

- Appreciates that the importance of feedback is to help people know whether they are on course, and how they are doing, and high performance is developed through a little-and-often approach of rewards and penalties

- Knows people do things for a reason, generally to do with the rewards they receive or penalties they avoid, and is consistent in their approach
- Makes full use of conditional feedback both positive and negative, and makes a point of catching people doing something right
- Understands that the greatest source of rewards a Leader-Developer has to offer is recognition in its various forms, and the most powerful reward they have to give is themselves. It is their I+U+ relationship built on trust with the individual which matters.
- Tells people, in advance, that they will be giving plenty of feedback, both positive and negative, in order to help people improve, and addresses the feedback to the behaviour, not personality or values
- Gives feedback as a powerful reward in its own sake, being an experience of recognition and praise which is relevant, real and central
- Is acutely aware of the reasons why people sometimes don't hear praise or criticism and knows how to deal with negative reactions

5

THE GEAR CHANGE: DEVELOPING STEP - TRANSFORMATIONAL LEADERSHIP

D1: Know Individual Needs and Motivations
Different strokes for different folks
Intrinsic and extrinsic motivation
Building blocks for motivation
Motivation Inventory: Understanding yourself and others
Motivation, learning and development
Transformational development and motivation

D2: Flexibly Adapt Style
How to be Situationally Consistent
The Directing, Mentoring, Coaching and Delegating Styles
Leadership style and rewards
Assessing development levels
Chapter summary

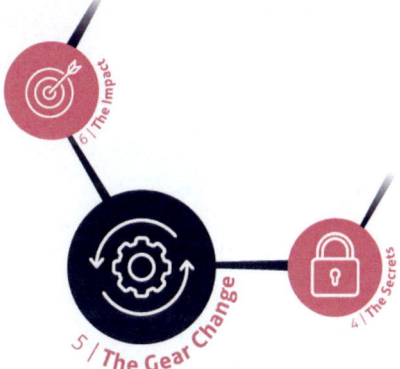

'I define a leader as anyone who takes responsibility for finding the potential in people and processes, and who has the courage to develop that potential.'
— Bréne Brown

D1: Know Individual Needs and Motivations

> Relate to team members as individuals; be realistic and knowledgeable about own and others' strengths and weaknesses; perceptive in knowing individuals' motivation patterns and needs, and skilled in providing appropriate rewards.

Different strokes for different folks

Each one of us has things in common with other people and, at the same time, we are all uniquely different. Effective Leader-Developers are perceptive to and recognise such individual difference, respond well to it (while remaining Situationally Consistent) and treat their people as individuals, including providing appropriate rewards and consequences to help them develop. Being perceptive to individual difference matters greatly in helping someone to succeed and grow. This applies particularly to the levels and direction of motivation the individual has.

What is motivation?

It is the factors which cause, channel and sustain an individual's behaviour, leading to appropriate levels of commitment and effort in the situation (or not). Some of these factors have to do with the individual. Some have to do with the situation they are in. A negative illustration of motivation is the Won't Do (as opposed to the Can't Do) syndrome discussed in Chapter 3 – get to the root of issues. In many ways, motivation is about 'will'.

All of us are likely to know people who are highly gifted in their natural abilities, and they possess skills and knowledge. However skilled they are, some have succeeded less well than others who seemingly have fewer natural abilities but who, nevertheless, have put their abilities to better use. This is typically down to someone's will to succeed. This highlights the importance of motivation in performance. Additionally, when we think about particular situations we have experienced, we can readily see that the situation itself, and the way we saw it, had a major effect on our approach to it. As individuals, we are likely to feel that we can (skills) and want to (motivation) cope much better with some situations than others, which can be represented like this:

Performance = (skills x motivation) situation

Working with individual differences

Becoming knowledgeable about the other person, discovering and connecting with the needs they have,

D1: KNOW INDIVIDUAL NEEDS AND MOTIVATIONS

really matters in 'fine-tuning' your approach to developing high performance, and more, in developing the person as a person. But it 'takes two to tango', and part of understanding the other person is in understanding yourself better. What follows should help in this also. The risk otherwise is seeing others just as an extension of yourself, with the same wants and needs, and perhaps on the basis that 'they should be just like me'. If this is the case then you won't make good contact.

> One real example of this is where a manager gave a team member the exciting but challenging project of relocating a technical library and, at the same time, reorganising it to make it more efficient. Its present location was such that people could readily stop by for a chat, and the systems and procedures had grown in a topsy-turvy way, without being thought through.
>
> The manager was highly enthusiastic about the opportunities involved when briefing the librarian. But nothing seemed to happen and the manager became increasingly irritated with the librarian's response, or lack of it.
>
> Finally, the penny dropped for the manager. He realised that he had been arrogant enough to assume that other people (and the librarian in particular) were like him, wanted the same

things, and were stimulated and motivated to achieve them. When he thought about it more, he realised that part of his motivation pattern was achievement and challenge (hence his enthusiasm for the project), while the librarian's was more concerned with social needs (he actually enjoyed the interruptions), security, and familiar ways of doing things.

The manager could see that he had presented what he thought was a marvellous opportunity to the librarian, but the librarian experienced it as a threat, not an opportunity. When he adjusted his approach to meet the motivational needs of the other person, things started to happen, and the project was completed well and on time.

Huge sums of money have been spent on researching motivation. There are no magic pills or formulas. What follows is a distillation of what is relevant to developing high performance, together with a powerful, practical tool for understanding patterns of Motivation.

Intrinsic and extrinsic motivation

Basically, motivation comes from within (intrinsic) or without (extrinsic). You know from the last chapter that intrinsic rewards are 'psychological' ones experienced directly by the individual, and extrinsic rewards are provided by an outside agent.

A simple example of extrinsic motivation would be a bonus for completing a piece of work on time. An example of intrinsic motivation is when someone sets themselves a challenging task for the sense of achievement its completion brings about for them. Another example could be influencing someone to a point of view, or helping them achieve their goals.

Sometimes, the same reward can be perceived by one individual to be extrinsic, while for another it will be intrinsic. The new car parked on the driveway may represent achievement and self-esteem in an intrinsic way, as well as material well-being. Equally, the cup of coffee a leader hands to a team member can be symbolic, as well as extrinsically material, in that it can be a form of recognition which connects with what is inside the person, say the celebration and thanks for a job well done.

What is important in this is that Leader-Developers:

- Recognise the power of intrinsic motivation
- Are highly alert to individual difference

The problem with extrinsic motivation is that the stimulus has to be fuelled from outside, and is rarely self-sustaining. For example, one sales manager we worked with led his team almost entirely by the extrinsic motivation of attending sales conferences for achievement. Initially, this worked very well, but it was not sustainable in the longer term and performance stabilised.

Meanwhile, another sales manager in the same company used intrinsic as well as extrinsic rewards. He led his team in such a way, that continued membership of the team became prized in itself, and each team member derived personal satisfaction from being party to the team's continued improvement. The performance of that branch came to far outstrip the other one.

With many organisations, too, the extrinsic rewards are set out by the organisation and are not influenced greatly by an individual leader. In such circumstances, once people are 'in' the organisation they can obtain many of these rewards by providing a mediocre level of performance only.

A problem with intrinsic motivation on the other hand is that needs may be 'buried', and are not visible to the individual or the leader. Habituation and situational factors all have an effect. The needs within a person may be dormant, suppressed or unrecognised until the right situation or stimuli are encouraged.

D1: KNOW INDIVIDUAL NEEDS AND MOTIVATIONS

In the performance development equation shared earlier, importantly, it is the leader who creates the situation, the context, whether this be a productive and fulfilling one, a neutral one or a counter-productive one.

One example of changing needs (or needs which were perhaps there but not released, rather like a spring held in compression) occurred in a Civil Service Department, which had to adapt to a new, initiative-taking culture as part of a move from its traditional format into a commercial business unit. This required staff to work in a more proactive and Interdependent way than before. The energy released was akin to the spring finding its natural form. Of course, this wasn't true for everyone, some found the move difficult because their source of motivation fitted with the old order of things, but a surprisingly large majority 'flowered' in the new situation.

It is intrinsic motivation that Leader-Developers concentrate on most. Their access to substantial extrinsic rewards is usually limited anyway. This is not to say that such extrinsic rewards don't matter, they do. The basic conditions and salary levels have to be perceived as reasonable otherwise they will act as a de-motivator. But it is the intrinsic ones which, generally speaking, are more powerful and sustainable in that the energy is released from within, not applied externally.

Lower and higher order needs

There are many generalised theories or models of motivation. The problem with generalised approaches is that individual differences in strength of need are difficult to determine. Nevertheless, they can give an overall perspective.

One of the best known of these approaches is Maslow's Hierarchy of Needs, and many of the other approaches are derived from this. Basically, the Hierarchy of Needs says:

- People have a number of needs, arranged as a hierarchy
- An individual is likely to be interested in fulfilling the next, higher, level of need in the hierarchy

D1: KNOW INDIVIDUAL NEEDS AND MOTIVATIONS

once their present one, and the need below it, have been largely satisfied

- The strength of a particular need will vary, individual to individual, but they all tend to apply to everyone in the order of importance shown

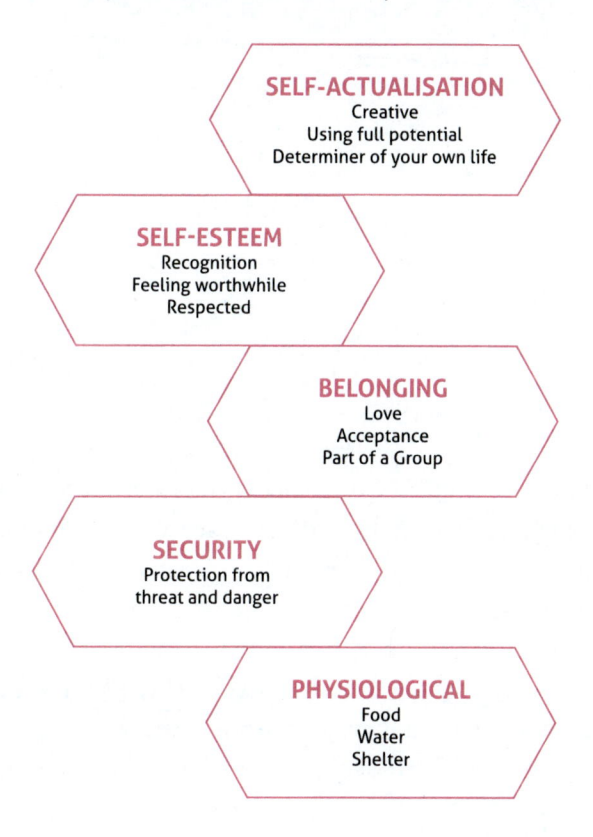

SELF-ACTUALISATION
Creative
Using full potential
Determiner of your own life

SELF-ESTEEM
Recognition
Feeling worthwhile
Respected

BELONGING
Love
Acceptance
Part of a Group

SECURITY
Protection from
threat and danger

PHYSIOLOGICAL
Food
Water
Shelter

Where do you feel you currently fit on this hierarchy and where are the members of your team? Are there any similarities?

The 'higher order' needs will be seen to be intrinsic ones, and the 'lower order' ones are extrinsic. Note how recognition and many of the rewards and motivations we have already talked about already fit in the hierarchy, and the importance of self-esteem.

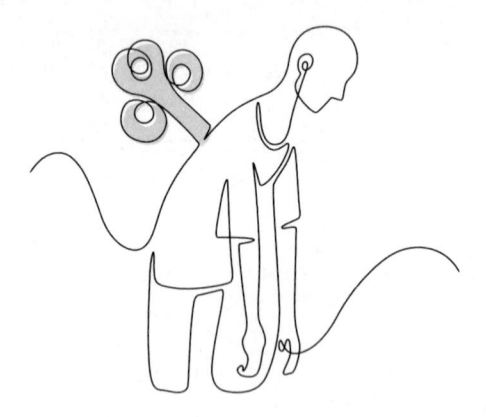

Both the strength of a particular need and the way it is perceived and actioned will vary with individuals, which means just relying on the hierarchy is limited in its usefulness. Money, for example, may mean security for some, for others self-esteem (eg the big car on the drive), for others it can mean self-actualisation (such as building an enterprise, with the money giving some measure of the achievement). Some people may have low security and high self-actualisation needs, compared with others who have the reverse.

Usually, Maslow is drawn as a pyramid. We have chosen to draw it as a tower of bricks, each one resting on the foundation of the one below it, so that if a lower one is removed, those above it fall down. Change, or threatened change, often has this effect on people, so they become particularly concerned with their needs for security, and often (temporarily) less concerned with the higher order needs. In this situation, people can sometimes be seen as behaving irrationally in their perception of the change, even though the change could benefit some of their higher order needs.

Building blocks for motivation

Effective Leader-Developers have developed their skill in setting the right situation or context for learning and growth. They have done this by focusing on the following building blocks because they know these are an important starting point when motivating others and building their self-esteem:

- **Have high expectations:** If your expectations about someone's performance are low or moderate, you will get just that. If your expectations are high (but not artificially or unrealistically so) you will tend to get that more. High Expectations are essential for the Challenge part of High Challenge-High Support.
- **Create goal focus and clarity:** This is where Explicitness is important. There is a direct relationship between goal clarity and motivation; if the goal isn't clear and felt worthwhile, motivation – even if high initially – won't

be sustained. Such a situation can even be experienced as stressful.

- **Build (realistic) self-esteem; make the performance level attainable:** Enable and facilitate an early success and celebrate and build on it. If people feel the goal they are being asked to pursue is too difficult or impossible, or the effort/rewards balance is not right, their motivation will be low. This fits with working in a series of smaller steps, reinforced at each stage with rewards or consequences appropriate to the individual.

- **Reinforce good performance:** Catch someone doing something right and encourage them to do more of the same, giving constant feedback.

- **Work to 'meta' goals:** Create a world to which people want to belong through vision and common purpose, so their energies and intrinsic motivation are engaged; developing in partnership with the person, providing the context so they can create their own success, and not just narrow task skills.

- **Provide High Support:** The necessary complement to High Challenge, but more than that, so that your relationship is valued, and you are seen as a trusted mentor.

- **Apply Situational Leadership:** This is concerned with flexing your style to each person's level of development. It will be described in more detail in the next section, as skill in this area is key and where The Gear Change is felt most acutely.

Motivation Inventory: Understanding yourself and others

One way to start thinking about the individual members of your team is to simply think about what they do/like best. Knowing the individual matters greatly.

A more comprehensive and complete way is through the Motivation Inventory which establishes, for an individual, their unique motivational patterns. The categories are shown on the following page. As you will see, although the factors are common (and provide a highly useful framework) it is the pattern and combination of the factors, and the relative weight placed on each one, that gives much insight. This brings us back to the notion that each one of us has things in common with other people but at the same time we are all uniquely different.

It is suggested that you use this framework to think about your own motivation patterns, because:

- To understand others you first need to understand yourself

- Appreciating individual differences enables you to better deal with people as individuals

Be honest with yourself in identifying the six most important statements for you – then, of the six, the two most important of all. After that, identify which statements are least important for you. Don't have in mind what you think you should be, but rather who you are.

Then think about other members of your team, perhaps two people who are 'different' from each other – maybe even someone you have some difficulty with, and see if you can identify the important differences between them and you.

People	
Influence	Persuading, communicating, developing; convincing people towards a course of action
Nurture	Helping people achieve their goals; listening to them; providing close support as well as time and attention
Gregariousness	Meeting and working with a wide range of people, including the public
Solitude	Having space to get on with things without contact or distraction from other people
Affiliation	Having close relationships; being part of a team; working interdependently with others and being liked and respected by them
Dedication	Helping the company's wider society and the community; doing something worthwhile; making the world a better place to be
Relating	Responding to different individual needs; dealing with difficult interpersonal situations; trusting and being trusted; resolving conflict

D1: KNOW INDIVIDUAL NEEDS AND MOTIVATIONS

Achievement	
Task focus	Having a liking for detail and analysis; using skills and knowledge; enjoying specific tasks, intellectual challenge; focusing on the job in hand
Goal Orientation	Working to targets; a future perspective to achieve tangible results; output rather than input focused; problem solving; satisfying customers and providing good service; achieving business results
Power and authority	Having control over others; being able to direct them and control work and events; making big decisions; being regarded as the source of authority
Responsibility	Leading others; taking and accepting responsibility for decisions; making a difference; doing what is necessary to ensure company success; representing others
Initiative and independence	Using own initiative; dislike of bureaucracy and red tape; operating independently; deciding own course of action
Creativity	Generating ideas; producing something new; finding new ways
Challenge	Being stretched; liking energy and hard work and competitive situations; responding to pressure and deadlines; being active and challenged

Enjoyment	
Suitability	Comfort in knowing capability to do job based on previous experience; perceived match of knowledge and skills
Structure	Operating to guidelines and systems; organising and planning; meeting standards; creating order, procedure and systems
Security	Job security; knowing what is going on; a liking for certainty
Tangible reward	Money; status; glamour; perks
Variety and fun	Enjoyment and fun; difference; travel; location; not repetitive or being bored
Recognition	Being well regarded and appreciated; feeling good about self and work; self-development
Comfort	Working moderate hours; not dealing with unpleasant or difficult situations; keeping clear of anxiety and stress; avoiding failure

Interpretation and review of categories

The first thing to do is to compare the overall balance between People, Achievement and Enjoyment. Effective Leader-Developers tend to have both high Achievement and People motivation (High Challenge for Achievement, High Support for People). Sufficient Enjoyment is required to enable people not to become overly stressed or to develop tunnel vision.

Now start to explore the various factors within each general category. For example, it will soon be seen that the expression 'they are a people person' is meaningless. The person may have a strong orientation towards others, but is it to influence them or be liked, to dominate or support, to just be with people or to have deeper relationships with them?

In the world of work, having high People motivation is usually not enough by itself, it needs to be coupled with Achievement to secure movement, otherwise, it just becomes a social or friendship group with no Task Focus.

This can be illustrated by looking at the profile for a successful leader, who will have Goal Orientation rather than Task Focus, has high Responsibility needs (but not high Power and Authority ones), welcomes being able to use Initiative and Independence and actively wants Challenge. They will want to Influence people, be comfortable with working with a range of them, will have a team orientation without being submerged by the team, and will want to relate to team members, but not to the degree that they lose sight of the Achievement part of the equation.

There are other factors too. For example, the technical expert is likely to relish Challenge, applied with Task Focus where a prized skill can be used (Suitability) within a Structure. Another example would be the combination of high Structure and low Initiative and Independence needs, which tend to result in difficulty with being flexible and solving problems or people who are driven by High Challenge and low Suitability sometimes bite off more than they can chew. Equally, people who do not want to be distracted by others (Solitude) concentrating on the mixture high Task Focus without much need for Variety and Fun, can be worth their weight in gold in one context, and fearfully inappropriate in another.

This is where it is well worth understanding the different sources of People, Achievement and Enjoyment motivation. There is all the difference in the world, for example, between Task Focus and Goal Orientation; both are important forms of Achievement motivation, but they differ in kind.

Potential problems can occur when there is perhaps too little or too much of a particular type of motivation. For example, being overly high on Initiative and Independence can mean that the person is difficult to manage; being very low can result in Dependence. The opposite side of this coin is that ignoring a team member's need for Nurture can result in high stress; too much Nurture can smother. Remember too that there are no 'perfect' people – rather there are relative strengths and weaknesses for a particular job.

You will have noticed that many of these motivation factors, and the rewards that come with them, are intrinsic ones. They come from within the person, they are part and parcel of them, and the satisfaction of the need brings the reward – eg Challenge. They have more to do with what people put into the job – possibly of course, their manager encourages, facilitates and recognises this, largely through knowing the motivation pattern of the person. Other rewards are extrinsic, the stimulus is provided to the person, such as with Tangible Reward and Variety and Fun, and have more to do with what people 'get out' of the job.

In this connection, if the motivation pattern is one of low People and Achievement motivation, and extremely high Enjoyment requirements – such as high pay, much glamour and status, fun, variety and travel, with little challenge and hard work – the expectation may be a little unrealistic, particularly in today's world. It is sometimes a characteristic of people who are strongly dissatisfied with their jobs, or series of jobs.

One of the advantages of frameworks such as the Motivation Inventory is that they enable you to think more clearly about not only yourself, but the people you work with. Within your group there will be similarities as well as differences; being perceptive about the differences will help in adjusting your approach, style and even rewards, to different people. It is a case of different strokes for different folks while monitoring your Situational Consistency.

It is important, too, not to let your own profile, or prejudices even, blind you to the difference in others. Because you are one person, with a particular set of primary sources of motivation, it does not mean that those who differ from you are wrong, but just different, often with the richness that this can bring. Above all, to understand others, the first person who must be understood is you.

Effective Leader-Developers understand their highest motivators need to be in the People and Achievement categories, and must work on ways to ensure their own needs are met, so they become the best leaders of people they can be.

Motivation, learning and development

The way we approach situations such as change and learning is strongly influenced by The Mindset we have. We have stressed that the particular 'lens' through which Leader-Developers see their world is crucial to their effectiveness as Leader-Developers and that the truly successful ones operate to the principle of both High Challenge and High Support. In this sense it is the leader who defines the situation and, if they are successful, it helps the team members to redefine it for themselves. Such redefinitions, or shifts in mindset, are the crucial part of real, continual and sustained learning and development.

The Mindset of the command-and-control system of managing (which many of us have been subject to, or have applied) was useful perhaps in many previous situations, but only up to a point. It is not the way to cause the 'meta' vision of people performing at their very best to happen, and it is certainly not the way to enable people to use their initiative responsibly and well. It is sometimes said that the Transactional Skills used in the Mobilising Step of *The Liberator* process, are those of the classic reinforcement approach – stimulus, response, reinforcement – and concentrate on behaviour change only, and that is to some extent true. But such a Transactional approach is necessary to realise a satisfactory level of performance. Then there are situations where it is important to prescribe and reinforce the right way – safety and some operating procedures being a case in point. It is an integral part of the journey towards the Developing and Enabling Steps, which constitute the Transformational part of the whole High Challenge-High Support approach.

Dolphins and learning leaps

Rather than envisioning people like pigeons, or computers even, porpoises and dolphins provide much more respectful and appropriate insights for understanding human behaviour. Again, this is not to say that people are dolphins, it is simply that because dolphins are studied in ways that people are not, the results provide a useful way of understanding certain forms of learning. Next to humans, porpoises and dolphins are regarded as the most intelligent beings, their creativity and ability to use discretion and judgement is remarkable.

It is the exercise of creativity and discretion – doing what is right at the time – that Transformational Leaders seek to develop in their people, to equip them for the rigours of today's world. This is achieved through the Developing and Enabling Steps of The Process and leads to Independence and Interdependence.

Research involving the training of dolphins has shown that:

- They are extremely sensitive to the context of their training; why they are doing it and with whom

- They are extremely sensitive to their relationship with the trainer (Leader-Developer)

In order to effectively train a dolphin you must establish a relationship with it, otherwise it will ignore you – even if you are the one who feeds it. In an organisational setting, 'feeding' is represented by pay, and the relationship has to be more than just being the hierarchical leader; a relationship built on Personal Power, Positive Regard, Genuineness and Trust will be necessary. Also necessary will be some identification with the reasons and purpose of the training – ie that it is legitimate.

Some other relevant findings were:

- Occasionally the dolphin became increasingly disturbed and frustrated at being 'wrong' and the trainer found it necessary to give the dolphin an unearned fish to preserve the relationship, for

D1: KNOW INDIVIDUAL NEEDS AND MOTIVATIONS

if the dolphin became too frustrated with the trainer it would refuse to co-operate. Here we can extrapolate the need for continued support and encouragement, not punishment, in times of difficulty and when the situation is high Will Do, low Can Do, and also the importance of maintaining the effort/reward balance through achievable steps.

- Sometimes dolphins would go wild with excitement, putting on an elaborate performance, including displaying some completely original behaviours, having made a 'breakthrough'. It had put things together for itself (in non-dolphin dialect 'the penny had dropped') and there was a thrill in the learning that needed to be caught and celebrated. In the organisation setting it matters greatly that the Leader-Developer is a partner in catching and celebrating that 'breakthrough'. This 'break through' was connected with the third, and crucially important point below, it had learned 'classes' of behaviour, not just behaviour.

- Classes of behaviour are different from a particular behaviour in that the connections, or learning, came from the dolphin (or person) themselves. It is learning to learn, not just responding to a particular stimulus or reward, where the learning of new tasks gets faster and faster, particularly when they fall into the same class of activity, enabling 'learning leaps' to be made.

Level I and Level II Learning

There are at least two types of learning, which we will call Level I and Level II.

LEVEL I	LEVEL II
Based on stimulus, response, reinforcement, so that behaviour is changed through the Transactional actions of the Leader-Developer, such as the Mobilising stage of The Liberator Process.	Learning to recognise the larger context in which the stimulus is occurring so its meaning can be correctly interpreted. This requires a will, or motivation to learn, such motivation coming from the person themselves.

Learning leaps have to do with learning changes of behaviour. Clearly, the ability to learn patterns this way involves more than simple stimulus, response, and reinforcement sequences for isolated behaviours, and involves attitudes as well as skills and behaviours. Although Level II does involve reinforcement, it is of a different type than simple reinforcement for task learning. The reinforcement is for 'exploration', that is, in using Responsible Initiative in trying new things out.

Transformational development and motivation

The ability to explore, to learn to exercise Responsible Initiative and judgement, or to be creative, is a higher level of learning than the specific behaviours which make up these abilities, not least because they involve attitudes or mindsets and not just behaviours. The processes and dynamics at this level are Transformational, for the Steps in The 4-Step Process are the Developing and Enabling ones, and they require a quality of relationship between the Leader-Developer and the team.

- **Developing and Enabling involves:**
  - Creating a world to which people want to belong, which they relate to with commitment and not just compliance, where the driving force is their own internal motivation

- **Leader-Developers who are effective in the Developing and Enabling Steps:**
  - Use Transformational Skills as well as Transactional ones
  - Establish productive, trusted relationships with their people
  - Encourage Level II Learning opportunities

- Work at the level of mindset or attitudes as well as behaviour
- Continue to provide supportive feedback which reinforces the internal motivation of the individuals
- Provide a context in which it is safe to learn
- Maintain High Challenge as well as High Support

- **Their aim is to help equip their people to:**

  - Operate Interdependently using Responsible Initiative
  - Take responsibility for their own continuous learning and development

Here the role of the Leader-Developer is to create and manage the context and relationship in which people can excel instead of simply telling them what to do. The thrust becomes not to 'condition' specific behaviours, but rather to get the person to be creative within their own natural set of behaviours. The success of the Leader-Developer is based on their ability to 'draw out' or release the potential abilities of the person. This involves encouraging the person to learn to generate new behaviours on their own, within the boundaries and context of the task to be performed. The Leader-Developer here is not some uninvolved

D1: KNOW INDIVIDUAL NEEDS AND MOTIVATIONS

distant observer, but rather is part of the situation, relating to the person and genuinely wanting them to succeed, and having set the High Challenge maintains a relationship of High Support.

Feedback is still important, but the context and underlying message of this feedback is:

> You are in a situation in which it is safe to learn and to challenge yourself. The amount that you can learn and grow depends on your own initiative. It's OK to try new things and make mistakes. Nothing bad will happen to you if your mistakes are genuine ones. What is most important is that you do your personal best, and continually develop your ability, flexibility and professional mastery so that you become 'the best you can be'. You will be assisted and helped by supportive feedback.

What is supportive feedback in this situation? It is information to the person, based on observation about particular behaviours, coupled with motivation and meaning – what was liked about the behaviour – to encourage the person to do more of it and to continually search for ways to improve.

Feedback provides motivation when the information is made more meaningful through the individual being able to connect it with what they have done and make sense of it. Here the power of the motivation is not the outside stimulus or a material reward, the motivation is internal, the reinforcement being that the feedback gives meaning to what has been done and the reward comes from the individual themselves.

There is another type of feedback too which is important at this stage. This is the 'unearned fish' or positive comments, such as the unconditional praise or encouragement which supports and maintains the all-important relationship between the two people. All this of course is part of continuing support.

However, High Support by itself can create an illusion of success only because everything can be seen as positive. This is where it is so important to keep the High Challenge-High Support balance right, but, and it is an important but, one also where the team member increasingly participates in creating challenging situations for themselves that lead to this growth. This is part and parcel of people taking responsibility for their own learning and development, continuous improvement and becoming self-directing.

This is what Level II Learning is all about. It has to do with becoming enabled, to do what is required using Responsible Initiative in the fast-moving situations of today, where flexibility and coping with new and perhaps unfamiliar situations is so important. Of course, if a particular procedure needs to be followed, perhaps for safety or operational reasons, then a Level I approach focused on the explicit behavioural level of what the person is required to do, may be appropriate. But usually, having the 'end in mind' at the start of the whole process, the vision of seeing people becoming 'the best they can be', required people to take on the habits and approach of being Interdependent, not Dependent or Counter-Dependent – in short, using Responsible Initiative.

For this to be caused to happen, or allowed to happen in some cases, Level II Learning has to be encouraged and sustained, which involves self-motivated activity on the part of the learner. This is the key, the Transformational trigger that the really effective Leader-Developers work towards, action and achieve.

D2: Flexibly Adapt Style

Deal with individuals on the basis of what they do, not who they are; everyone knows clearly where they stand and that particular behaviours are responded to in consistent, particular ways; be Situationally Consistent by flexibly adapting style to deal with various levels of performance and commitment to the overall vision.

How to be Situationally Consistent

Situational Consistency is concerned with the adjustment of style and approach by the leader in response to a particular situation. Used well and proactively, it also causes and creates new situations such as accelerated development or improved performance. Equally, if the style used is inappropriate, rigid or inconsistent, then it will have a negative impact on the team member's performance.

No one style is effective in all situations. If, for example, there is a sudden fire in the workplace then clear direct leadership (to the next exit) is likely to be effective; where to go for a drink after work will be open to the views of everyone involved.

Some of the factors which influence the situation are:

- **The leader's past experience and expectations:** If the leader has used a particular style in the past and it has worked well, then the tendency is for that leader to stick to that style, even though the situation changes, instead of responding flexibly to the new situation. Also, a self-fulfilling prophecy applies in that if the leader expects low (or high) performance, the expectations will influence the results.

- **The leader's expectations and behaviour:** People tend to model themselves on their own leaders, and such leaders have much influence on people reporting to them. Change programmes often fail because although senior managers espouse new behaviours, they sometimes fail to carry them out themselves.

- **Peers' expectations and behaviour:** For example, whether peers operate in competition or co-operation.

- **Organisational culture and policies:** 'The way things are done around here.' The general direction is a move from a command and control culture to a more enabling one. This sometimes creates difficulties for leaders who lack the flexibility to adjust their styles or are actually more at home with command and control.

- **Task requirements:** Jobs that require precise instructions and the following of exact procedures (eg quality inspection) require a leadership style that will differ say, from that required for jobs where the way they are carried out can vary, or where discretion can be used (eg customer service).

- **Team members' characteristics, expectations and behaviour:** The Skills and Attitudes of team members also influence the leader's choice of style. The starting position may be that highly capable members require a less directive approach. Also, while some people want to be directed, others prefer taking responsibility for their own work.

Whatever the starting position, it is not necessarily fixed for all time, the situation is open to influence by the leader – as will now be discussed.

Situational Consistency, defined more clearly, is about the leader's skill in:

> selecting the right style for the situation
> (STYLE EFFECTIVENESS)

THE LIBERATOR

and

using an appropriate range of styles matched to the situation
(STYLE FLEXIBILITY)

as this results in

SITUATIONAL CONSISTENCY

To do this well requires an understanding of the individual, as an individual, and what might be called their 'maturity' in terms of the way they go about and approach their job role. In looking at 'maturity', where they are on the Dependency through to Interdependency voyage also matters greatly.

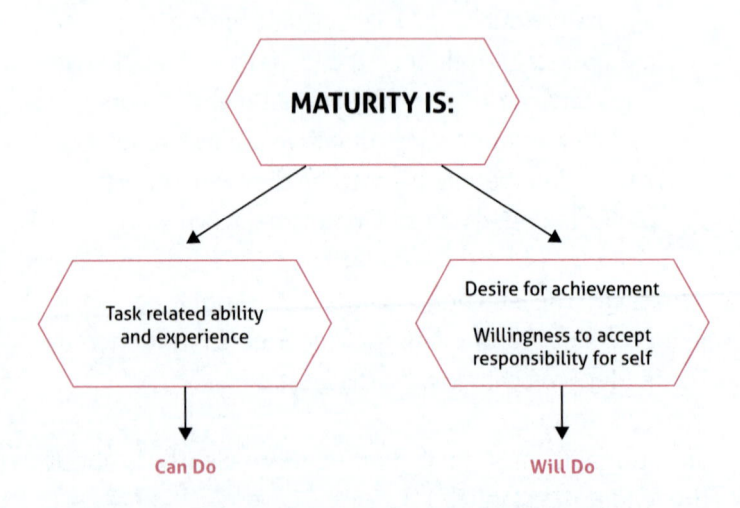

MATURITY IS:

Task related ability and experience

Can Do

Desire for achievement

Willingness to accept responsibility for self

Will Do

The Can Do/Can't Do and Will Do/Won't Do syndrome was described previously in Chapter 3.

One way of looking at Situational Consistency is through the following model, which serves also as an alternative way of viewing The 4-Step Process, to help cement your learning.

LEADERSHIP STYLES & SITUATIONAL CONSISTENCY SUMMARY

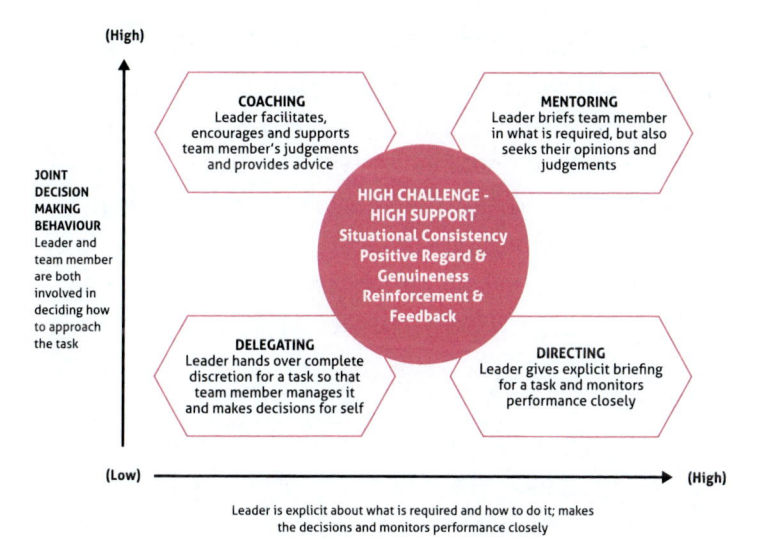

(High)

JOINT DECISION MAKING BEHAVIOUR
Leader and team member are both involved in deciding how to approach the task

COACHING
Leader facilitates, encourages and supports team member's judgements and provides advice

MENTORING
Leader briefs team member in what is required, but also seeks their opinions and judgements

HIGH CHALLENGE - HIGH SUPPORT
Situational Consistency
Positive Regard & Genuineness
Reinforcement & Feedback

DELEGATING
Leader hands over complete discretion for a task so that team member manages it and makes decisions for self

DIRECTING
Leader gives explicit briefing for a task and monitors performance closely

(Low) ⟶ (High)

Leader is explicit about what is required and how to do it; makes the decisions and monitors performance closely

Based on Blanchard, Zigarmi & Zigarmi 1985

The Directing, Mentoring, Coaching and Delegating Styles

Here there are four basic styles, or phases – phases in the sense that as team members develop and 'mature' the leader adapts their style to meet the new 'situation'. The first style is called Directing, where the leader gives explicit briefing for a task and monitors performance closely. The Skills of Explicitness and Assertion come very much into play here and, in fact, Directing is the style most appropriate to the Mobilising Step of *The Liberator* approach (Chapter 2).

Directing

Directing, as a style, can be appropriate initially for someone new to the team or organisation, where that person is unfamiliar with the organisation and the way things are done or unfamiliar with the task. A nondirective style here might cause anxiety and confusion, as it also might where major change is being carried out. The directness in these situations can provide the comfort of 'knowing where you are' which was illustrated earlier by the 'skating in the dark on top of a skyscraper' analogy.

Of course, directness does not imply a lack of Positive Regard, or discourtesy. There is, however, a trap to look out for. This is causing the team member to become dependent on you to always tell them what to do, particularly with people who are inclined or habituated towards Dependency anyway. Overuse of this style, without moving to others, can encourage such Dependency.

One other situation where the Directing style can be highly appropriate is in the performance issue of Can't Do, or Won't Do, or perhaps a combination of both. Facing, dealing with and resolving such issues usually requires directness, not through 'bawling out' or admonition, but in the ways previously described.

Mentoring

The next style in sequence is the Mentoring one, where the leader briefs the team member on what is required, but also seeks their opinions and judgements. The leader still provides guidance, and they also provide explanations and opportunities for clarification and suggestions. Both the leader and the team member are involved in deciding how to approach the task, although it is the leader, with this style, who finally decides the course of action.

Mentoring is used increasingly when the leader becomes satisfied that the person largely has the capability to do what is required and some willingness to do so. This style is used to encourage further efforts on the part of the team member and to demonstrate trust and support, even though they may not be ready or able yet to accept full responsibility for the task. Because it is 'involving', Mentoring is also a good learning style as it promotes active learning (instead of the passive learning of the Directing style) through a structure of guidance, with the safety net of the leader keeping a close eye on results. When the situation moves to a first flowering of Can Do and Will Do, it is the style to use, so it fits, as does Coaching, in a more advanced way, with the Developing Step of the whole approach.

Coaching

In the third phase, the Coaching phase, the team member's ability and motivation to take responsibility has increased, or is such already that the leader facilitates, encourages and supports the team member's judgement and provides advice, rather than the more directive guidance of the Directing and Mentoring Styles. Indeed, close direction is likely to be resented.

However, the leader will still need to provide High Support, recognition and encouragement if the fourth stage is to be achieved. For at this Coaching stage, although the Can Do may be high, there still may be wrinkles in the learning to achieve professional mastery, and the Will Do may need to be underpinned by greater self-confidence.

Delegating

The fourth stage is Delegating. We would actually prefer to call it Enabling or Enabled Delegation because it rarely happens by itself. Here, the leader hands over complete discretion for a task, so that the team member manages it and makes their own decisions because they are now self-directing, experienced and confident. They are on

D2: FLEXIBLY ADAPT STYLE

their own, flying solo – but they are not alone – you, the leader, are there providing not interference but backup, encouragement, recognition and continued support, dealing with mistakes as learning opportunities rather than as a chance to demonstrate that you knew best all along.

It is your style which alters, not the underlying framework of High Challenge-High Support you operate to with its high expectations, Positive Regard, regular feedback and reinforcement. You have delivered this throughout and will continue to do so even when the person is able and willing to operate to Enabled Delegation. The leader's task is now to sustain the team member there and help them grow further, not just to manage 'by exception' – that is, only giving feedback (negative) when a mistake is made and giving no recognition apart from that.

Applying the appropriate style according to how individuals behave in terms of their Can Do and Will Do capability and preparedness is Situational Consistency – or giving the same kinds of 'strokes to different folks' for the same kind of behaviour and doing so consistently and thoroughly. This also applies to the range of tasks an individual is required to perform; in one task someone may be at the Coaching stage, while at another, which is completely unfamiliar to them, the Directing style would be more appropriate.

If the leader is Situationally Consistent then the team member will know how the leader operates (the 'rules of engagement', so to speak), and the use of different

249

styles for different tasks where the level of competence varies, will not present problems – rather it will be experienced as helpful and facilitating.

Leadership style and rewards

Clearly, there is a strong connection between leadership style and the rewards you give. Being trusted, being given responsibility, using one's own judgement, receiving praise, and developing skills are examples of rewards and recognition for many people (but not all). Equally, the same rewards can be experienced as a threat, or even punishment, by others – such as might be the case in someone lacking in self-confidence who you would like to take more responsibility and be more self-directing. Or perhaps one of your team members is struggling to cope with change and is stuck at a particular stage in the Transition Curve. In such cases, the steps taken may need to be more gradual and reinforced with greater support. Generally speaking, though, people tend to welcome increased control of what they do at work.

On occasions, it will be legitimate to revert back to an earlier style. Sometimes this will happen when you have mistakenly overestimated someone's 'maturity', such as when their Can Do is not as well developed as you originally thought. Reverting to the previous style will rectify the situation and can be more helpful, for the time being, to the team member. (Make sure that you don't get stuck with or encourage Dependency, however.)

Flexing your leadership style can also be used to give penalties or consequences as well as rewards. If someone has been trusted with responsibility, say, through a Delegating or Coaching style, and that trust is used irresponsibly, then the 'punishment' could be to take away much of that responsibility, for the time being, by reverting to a Mentoring or Directing style. Or if someone has, perhaps after much effort, started to carry out a new task to your satisfaction so that you start to use a Mentoring instead of a Directing style, and for a while, they are fine but then their standards start to slip, you may need to get them back on course by some Directing. When the issue is a Won't Do and not a Can't Do, then it is a reprimand situation, and the penalty may include being supervised more closely.

Putting leadership style to work

We suggested earlier that a useful way of looking at Performance was through seeing it as the sum of the skills, motivation and the situation – or another way of looking at it is:

Performance = (Can Do × Will Do) Situation

In this, the situational factors matter greatly and include those factors, described earlier, which relate to the job such as task requirements, organisational culture and policies, etc. The match between the level of skills required for the job in its entirety, and the degree of discretion built into it, is all-important. For example, a nurse in an operating theatre will be required to carry out set procedures, while a customer services representative may be required to use much more individual discretion and initiative in handling certain situations. Having said this, the nurses who do carry out the set procedures with Responsible Initiative and who have a strategic view, progress the fastest – this is the focus of our earlier book, *The Pioneer*.

How team members perceive and define a situation, will depend on their expectations, past experiences, attitudes and characteristics. For example, one person may see an opportunity while another sees the same situation as a threat. In a situation of change, one team member may be stuck in a passive resistance mode while another is adapting well to that new situation. As part of the perception of the situation, too, the effort-reward bargain will be taken into account – that is, individuals come to a view as to whether they want the reward (or avoidance of consequences) sufficiently to put in the effort required.

The situation as the leader defines it

Leadership Style is very much to do with how the leader defines the situation, and their past experience and expectations, and perhaps the expectations of their manager,

D2: FLEXIBLY ADAPT STYLE

can have a major influence. For example, a leader may not believe in Enabled Delegation, preferring to be strongly Directing, or may not look at Style Flexibility and Skill to adjust style appropriately. The leader then becomes locked into a narrow way of operating, which in turn influences the way the situation is perceived by them.

A common style profile, in the UK at least, is often a diluted Coaching one, backed up by Mentoring, even when the situation plainly calls for a Directing or Delegating approach, or even the ability to switch appropriately, with Situational Consistency, between all four.

Effective Leader-Developers understand that, to achieve the greatest success for their teams:

- The situation is not passive or fixed
- As leader, they can change the situation
- They create the situation for the team's success

There are several levels to this, which relate to leadership style and Situational Consistency. One style, which you may have come across, leads to a low or poor level of effectiveness, where the style used is rigid or inappropriate, where nothing is ever changed, or attention and feedback (negative) are only given when things go wrong. The behaviour here is mistakenly believed to amount to delegation.

The other levels, more positively, give rise to effective performance, and when effective Leader-Developers build their skill in this, they know they have to employ both Transactional and Transformational leadership, described first in Chapter 2.

Transactional Leadership

This is the fundamental level. Transactional Leadership identifies what team members need to do to achieve the organisational goals, consider the situation, and help their people to be competent and confident in achieving such goals. The leader will judge what kind of style is appropriate for a particular situation, taking into account the 'maturity' of the skill and motivation of team members, their individual needs and their dignity. As part of this latter, they will flex their approach to synchronise well with the individual. For example, someone who is knowledgeable and long-serving might expect to be treated more like a peer than a subordinate.

Such Transactional Leadership, when it is carried out well, will be flexible and at the same time Situationally Consistent. It requires perception and the recognition that no one style is suitable for all situations, and the leader who wants to develop people so that they learn their work and increase their confidence and competence, will have to adapt their style consistently.

All this matters even at this level of leadership; it is straightforward, every day and, essentially, action based. There is another way of looking at leadership, however, in which the leader defines the situation in a wider and more powerful way.

Transformational Leadership

Transformational Leadership motivates us to do more than we originally expected to do. It does this by raising the sense of the importance and value of our tasks, by connecting us to the interests of the team and organisational purpose, and by raising the consciousness of our higher order, intrinsic needs. It differs in degree from Transactional Leadership in that it employs a higher degree of vision. Vision has to do with creating images of future goals, while action has to do with immediate behaviours.

THE LIBERATOR

Style characteristics and when to use them

DIRECTING	
Characteristics of the Directing style	Here the leader is very explicit about what is to be done and how it is to be done, and works very closely with a team member who is inexperienced about the particular task, or does not have the 'will' to carry it out well. The team member is allowed little discretion. • The leader knows precisely how the work is best carried out • Very detailed instructions are given by the leader • There is little or no room for the team member to use discretion • The work is closely monitored, with each stage checked and corrected before the next stage • All decisions are made by the leader
When to use the Directing style	• The team member has a low level of competence in the task or a low level of 'will do' • When mistakes, such as with safety, quality etc, cannot be left to chance • To get team members off to a fast start with new tasks • When the right habits need to be formed from the beginning
Tips in applying the Directing style	• Explain why you are using this style and how you are subsequently likely to use other styles which allow more involvement • Maintain Positive Regard and the team member's self-esteem; you are using this style to help them in the particular situation • Be explicit, clear and direct, breaking up the 'Direction' into manageable chunks • Give reasons/explanations why you want things carried out in a certain way • Reinforce good performance - catch people doing something right - and be ready to move to the next stage

D2: FLEXIBLY ADAPT STYLE

MENTORING	
Characteristics of the Mentoring style	Here the team member has a good basic understanding of what is required, and importantly wants to do it well or perhaps with more confidence, and is ready to take on more responsibility for simple decisions involved in the task. • The leader involves the team member more in how the task is to be done, moving away from just telling and explaining, to seeking opinions or getting the team member to start to exercise judgement. At the same time, the leader retains sufficient control to prevent significant mistakes and to keep overall direction • The leader does not closely supervise the basic task but requires to be kept fully involved in the decision making process • The leader encourages the team member to make suggestions about how to proceed or how to deal with particular problems • If there is disagreement on what should be done the leader makes the final decision
When to use the Mentoring style	• The team member has sufficient basic competence to be trusted to carry out the task and sufficient motivation (Will Do) to want to do it well • Judgement, discretion and Responsible Initiative are being used by the team member, but still need further development • The leader still has much more competence in the particular task than the team member and the transfer of that competence to the team member is some way from being complete • The team member lacks the confidence yet to 'fly solo', or perhaps is over-confident so that discretion is used irresponsibly
Tips in applying the Mentoring style	• Do not allow people to become Dependent on you (flattering though that may be), always push for suggestions from the team member about how to deal with issues • Ask for their opinions, give yours and explain any decisions when you override them • Be consistent in requiring to be kept informed; when people have demonstrated that they can be trusted to do what is required, tell them so • Don't revert to the Directing Style at the first Can't Do mistake • Provide lots of encouragement and support, use the Coaching Style clearly and strongly where the situation fits, and not as a 'cop out' for Directing

THE LIBERATOR

COACHING	
Characteristics of the Coaching style	This is the style to use when the team member has a good competence in the particular task, reasonable experience in it, and has consistently demonstrated high 'Will Do.' The team member can be trusted to deal with most issues without the intervention of the leader, but may still need, and feel the need for, direct support when difficult or unusual decisions are to be made, or where an unusual feature occurs which hasn't been experienced before by the team member. • The leader acts as a supportive 'colleague' in drawing out the team member's own ideas, helping by talking them through; being a sounding board • The leader makes observations or raises issues which need to be dealt with, but works to encourage team members to produce solutions • Decisions on routine matters are always made by the team member, decisions in new or difficult areas are made by joint problem solving • The leader positions team members to make good decisions by briefing them regularly on wider organisational issues
When to use the Coaching style	• The team member has good competence in the particular tasks, together with demonstrated judgement and high 'Will Do' • On those occasions where the team member has greater expert knowledge than the leader • Where the team member is capable of solving problems alone but sometimes needs encouragement and reassurance to feel confident in facing tough challenges • When the team member has sufficient competence and Will to try things out for self • Where the operating culture is already a 'collegiate' one, such is often the case with professional or knowledgeable workers, where the requirement on the leader is to be first amongst equals
Tips in applying the Coaching style	• Don't mistake control for accountability; because the leader is accountable for overall decisions, it does not mean Command and Control • Work to encourage team member's confidence in their own decisions, don't undermine them by suggesting you could always do it better • To learn making mistakes occasionally, except where carelessness is involved, treat mistakes as learning opportunities • Be more delighted when they can do it without you than when they need you (although always support willingly); your ego is less important than your team member's success.

D2: FLEXIBLY ADAPT STYLE

DELEGATING	
Characteristics of the Delegating style	This is not abdication, but a conscious clear recognition by the leader that with a particular piece of work, at least, the team member can do it, without any help, to a standard that is expert. The team member owns that part of the work, makes the decisions involved in it, is entrusted and empowered to make their own judgement and to use initiative responsibly. The leader withdraws from the operations part of the work, but with a firm understanding that the team member will keep them appropriately informed. The leader does not withdraw their support, however; the challenge belongs to the team member but the leader continues to provide strong, visible support in the background. It matters still to the leader that the team member is successful, more so than ever. • The leader leaves the team member completely free to deal with issues and make decisions for a particular piece of work, within an overall framework of parameters such as safety, budget requirements, etc • Although the leader does not require to be involved, they will require to be kept appropriately informed, such as with issues that impact other work, and to maintain their view of the big picture • The leader will still seek opportunities to recognise achievement and to maintain the relationship of support and encouragement
When to use the Delegating style	• Where there is both high 'Can Do' and 'Will Do' in a particular job area • To arrange more of the same • As a reward for those who demonstrate competence and willingness, and who are strongly motivated, intrinsically, to do good work • When the leader can usefully direct their own time to other important issues • When the requirements of the task are best suited to this style, eg customer service where each service opportunity needs to be tailored, within an overall framework, to the unique characteristics of the situation
Tips in applying the Delegating style	• Judge when the team member is ready for this style and tell them that they will take full charge of the piece of work from now on; you will have succeeded when you have enabled someone to operate in this truly empowered way • Give the team member the car keys, so to speak, and prize your own fingers off the steering wheel; don't interfere • If the team member asks too often, at first, for help, consciously push the decision back to them by asking what they would do

Assessing development levels

At any particular time, each team member, and also the team as a whole, will be at a particular stage of development for a particular task. It is important to be clear about what stage they are at so that you can be Situationally Consistent in the way you deal with them and also prepare for the next stage ahead.

The development level has two major components, which you will now be familiar with:

DEVELOPMENT LEVEL

CAN DO
Task Knowledge & Skills
Transferable Skills
Level II Learning

WILL DO
Motivation (External)
Motivation (Internal)
Confidence

When combined in varying amounts, Can Do and Will Do can be experienced as four levels of development for the particular task. These levels range from low, when the Directing style is appropriate, to high, when the Delegating style fits better.

In many ways, the Directing and Mentoring styles are 'Push' (directing someone to do something) styles, while the Coaching and Delegating styles are 'Pull' (the person taps into their own motivation to do it) styles. The crossover point, and what the Leader-Developer is seeking to achieve, is the switch to intrinsic motivation and its corresponding dynamic of Level II Learning. This is the Transformational stage, as has been described, where energy and commitment become their most powerful and what the most effective Leader-Developers always work towards.

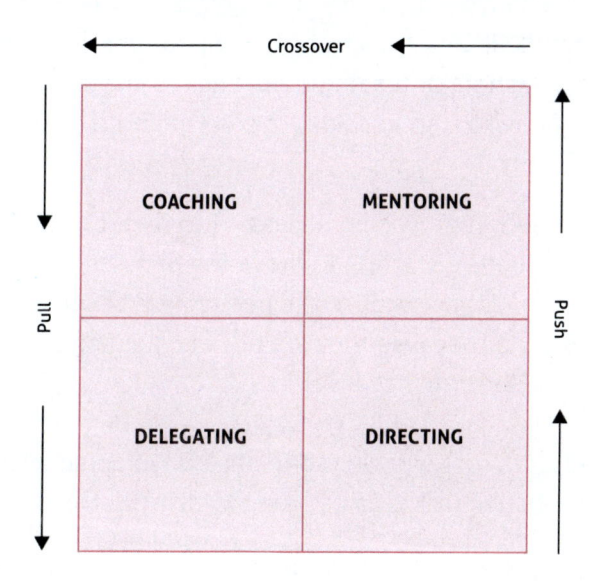

COACHING	MENTORING
DELEGATING	DIRECTING

Crossover

Pull

Push

In developing people through this approach, a number of points are especially important:

- It is the Will Do, that is the motivation, which is often the most important aspect as skills and knowledge are usually more readily trainable.

- When the Will Do becomes 'I really want to' – that is, the motivation comes from within the person themselves and not through some external reward or avoidance of consequences; Level II Learning really comes into its own and provides the continuing impetus; commitment is much stronger than compliance.

- Getting the balance right between putting too much on the team member before they can handle it, and thus setting them up for failure and frustration, or holding them back from stretching their wings, so to speak, is crucial – both can be equally damaging.

- Sometimes it will be necessary to revert back a step before starting to move the process forward again, either because the person wasn't quite ready or because they are not maintaining the new performance level.

A useful way of reviewing someone's development level at a particular task is to use the Maturity Matrix below:

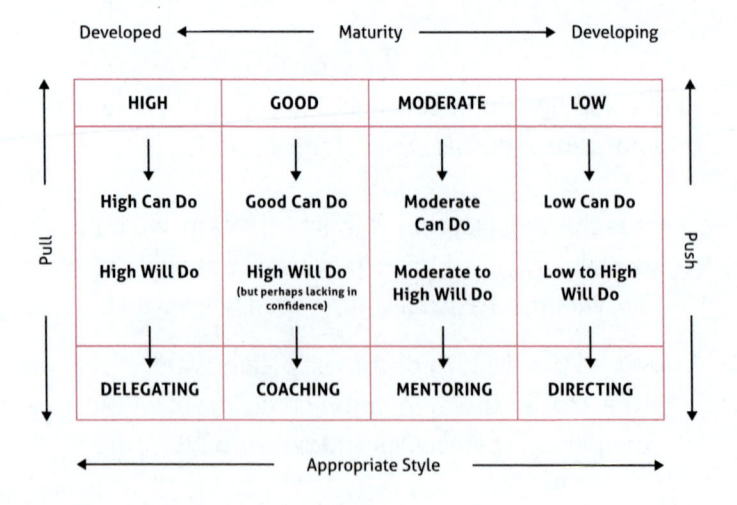

Developed ← Maturity → Developing

HIGH	GOOD	MODERATE	LOW
↓	↓	↓	↓
High Can Do	Good Can Do	Moderate Can Do	Low Can Do
High Will Do	High Will Do (but perhaps lacking in confidence)	Moderate to High Will Do	Low to High Will Do
↓	↓	↓	↓
DELEGATING	COACHING	MENTORING	DIRECTING

Pull ← → Push

← Appropriate Style →

Ask yourself the following questions when assessing the present state of the person, or team's, Can Do and Will Do. This will help you assess their current stage of development, for a particular task, on the Matrix.

Can Do	Will Do
• Do they understand what is required and that it is part of their job? • Have they received the appropriate training? • Do they have the skills and knowledge required? • Have they done the task successfully before? • Are they a Level I or Level II learner?	• Do they want to learn how to do the task? • Are they willing to take on the task? • Is there something 'in it' for them? • Are they prepared to accept responsibility for the result? • Are they a Level I or Level II learner? • Do they have the confidence to try out the task?

Chapter summary

D1: Know Individual Needs and Motivations

The Liberator:

- Understands that each one of us has things in common with other people but, at the same time, that we are all uniquely different. Being perceptive to individual differences matters greatly in helping someone to succeed and develop.

- Knows that motivation is what leads to effort in a situation, or not. In performance issues and development, it is usually motivation which matters most, often more so than Skills.

- Appreciates that different people have differing types and levels of motivation; real connection with a person is only made when their motivation pattern is understood.

- Starts by getting the right building blocks in place, which include setting expectations high, making the performance level attainable, working to meta goals and providing High Support.

- Is keenly aware there are no magic pills or potions, but there are ways to see what matters to the person and to respond to that. Motivation comes from within (intrinsic) or from without (extrinsic) a person. Extrinsic rewards first have to be reasonable, however.

- Like all effective Leader-Developers, concentrates on intrinsic motivation, knowing that it is more self-sustaining and leads to higher engagement and performance.

D2: Flexibly Adapt Style

The Liberator:

- Knows that no one style is effective in all situations. Effective Leader-Developers flex their style appropriately in response to, or cause, a particular situation, and they do so consistently.

- Understands that Situational Consistency is the ability of the leader to select the right style for the situation (Style Effectiveness), and to use an appropriate range of styles matched to the situation (Style Flexibility).

- Flexibly uses the four basic styles – Directing, Mentoring, Coaching and Delegating – all of which require High Challenge-High Support, with different expressions of this for each.

- Appreciates that most Leader-Developers have one or two primary preferred styles. It is useful to know what your bias is so that you can 'round out' your repertoire.

- Realises in the performance development equation – Performance = (Can Do x Will Do) Situation – that it is the Leader-Developer who defines the situation. Effective Leader-Developers create the situation for the team's success.

- Employs Transformational Leadership to motivate us to do more than we originally expected we could do. They are skilled Enablers, who inspire Level II Learning and the engagement of intrinsic motivation.

6

THE IMPACT

The Test: Leading Change and Transition
Leading change through *The Liberator* approach
The Change Transition Curve
The Marathon Effect
Change and performance gain or loss
Preparing yourself to lead change
Intensity of effort
Checklist: 'How I deal with change'
The Review: Putting It All Together
The Liberator Wheel
Chapter summary

'When the effective leader is finished with his work, the people say it happened naturally.'
— Lao Tse

The Test: Leading Change and Transition

Leading change through *The Liberator* approach

The premise of *The Liberator* approach is that, if you are using The Mindset of High Challenge-High Support in powerful and equal combination, working through The 4-Step Process appropriate to your people's individual stages of development, and deploying the full power of The Skills when needed, you will be fit to lead change well. This is The Test for you, and this chapter will help you to know where you need to place your developmental energies if there is more work to be done.

The Liberator is concerned with bringing about necessary and planned change. Planned, in that it is 'visioned' and led through The Process and stages described, as a series of digestible steps – sometimes called Incremental Change or Continuous Improvement. It is necessary because, in today's world, high performance is the route to both personal and organisational survival. One of the features of high-performing teams is that they deal with change with vigour and resolution as a new challenge, buttressed by support, confident and capable of doing what is required.

It is not surprising that such teams respond this way for they have acquired, through the actions of the Leader-Developer, the habits of being enabled – Continuous Improvement, Level II Learning and the ability to use their initiative responsibly. Organisational change, almost inevitably, is in the direction of these skills and habits, which are the very essence of successful adaptation and growth. Leader-Developers who secure such high-performing teams are not only dealing with today's needs but preparing for those of tomorrow. For change is inevitable and certain, and those people and organisations who cope best with it have become well versed in its 'rules of engagement' and know they have the capacity to cope.

The last decade or so has been a decade of change for most organisations, and that change has often been turbulent rather than the more controlled incremental approach of yesteryear. And the future is looking no less turbulent. The only certainty is that there will be further waves of change, just as sea waves roll in from beyond the horizon – some gentle, others threatening, with the occasional unpredictable rogue wave, larger and more devastating than the rest.

Some organisations, and individuals within them, have 'surfed' such waves of change well, harnessing their power and energy, while others have bobbed about in the backwash like jetsam. Still others, denying the existence of such waves, turned their back to them only to receive a cold, sharp shock when a wave, larger than the rest, caught them unawares.

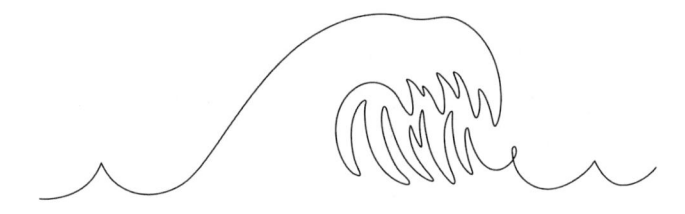

Incremental and step change

Change, whether it is incremental or a more major step change is likely to continue. Managing in a constantly changing environment requires the high-performing competencies we have talked about because these are crucial for surviving and prospering in today's world.

Incremental, continuous change, generally speaking, works better than step change, and incremental, continuous change (sometimes called Transformational change) comes through *The Liberator* processes which have been described.

Sometimes though, the situation or the organisation requires step change which is larger and more sudden than the incremental approach. Typically, step change is large-scale and organisation-wide, such as:

- Downsizing – 'cutting out the fat'
- Flattening the structure – eliminating middle management positions
- Decentralising corporate staff functions
- Introducing a 'new' culture
- Business process re-engineering

However, *The Liberator* principles and processes still apply, often more strongly than ever, because:

- Change means new competencies (Skills and Behaviours) have to be accepted, developed and mastered
- Explicitness in what is required helps enormously (remember the story about roller skating on top of a tall building in the dark?)
- Every change will have some spin-off of unintended consequences which will need to be spotted and dealt with
- High Challenge (which is how change can be interpreted) will lead to stress and random development and performance unless accompanied by High Support

Challenge and support in leading change mastery

The last point deserves particular emphasis because there is a process we all go through when encountering change, whether it be a new job or whether we need to respond to a new situation of change. Sometimes it is a matter of days before people effect the transition, sometimes years. Sometimes people get stuck and never successfully complete the transition (which is painful and debilitating). Also, people go through the process at different rates or can regress, which can be confusing for the unprepared Leader-Developer. The Leader-Developer has a key role in all this by providing the support necessary, but the kind of support required will vary according to what stage of the process the person has reached.

The Change Transition Curve

The process, or Transition Curve, is shown below, with the two axes being the feeling of Competence/morale (being able to cope, a preparedness to make the effort to cope) and Time. Feelings matter a great deal when people are moving through the Transition Curve and, as well as labelling each stage with a one-word description of behaviour, the underlying mindset (using the language of the OK Corral described earlier) has also been included.

The change curve

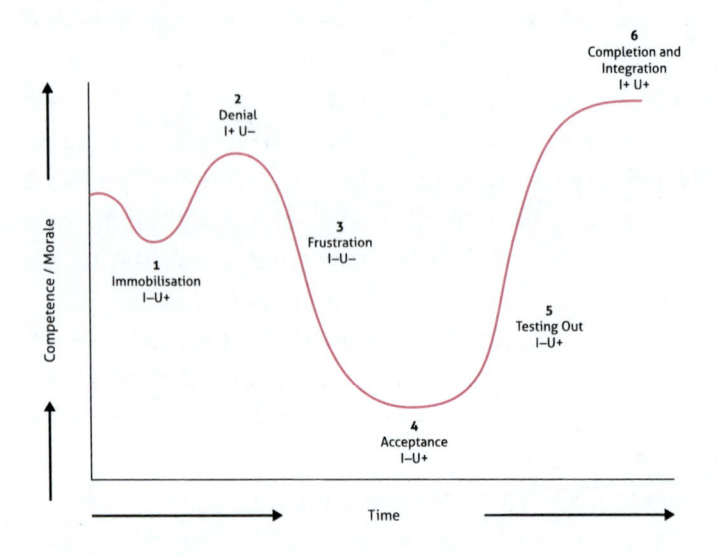

[Figure: Change curve graph showing Competence/Morale vs Time, with six stages:
1 Immobilisation I–U+
2 Denial I+ U–
3 Frustration I–U–
4 Acceptance I–U+
5 Testing Out I–U+
6 Completion and Integration I+ U+]

From a personal point of view, while understanding and accepting this natural reaction does not affect the change, it does help us to cope and rise to the challenges presented by the change more productively.

This understanding also makes our dealings with others who are experiencing change, and who are therefore on the curve, more supportive and helps them survive and thrive.

The stages of the curve:

- **Stage 1** is typified by shock, temporary disbelief and a sense of immobilisation. Even a positive change can elicit this response – in the sense of not believing your good luck.

Imagine the response of a major winner in the National Lottery!

- **Stage 2** is a denial that they are affected by the change. The individual attempts to shrug off the change and continue as if nothing had happened. It is possible for some people to get stuck at this stage, in which case the wave of change will eventually swamp them.

- **Stage 3** is the downward slope of powerlessness and frustration. It is an inevitable and necessary stage during which people can experience a whole range of emotions, such as grief, rage and fear. Behaviour can be irrational, and this is not a time to make major decisions. To help someone who is experiencing this stage, it is best to just support and accept the feelings – logic has little use here.

- **Stage 4** gives way to an acceptance of the situation. The person can feel drained and resigned after the emotion of Stage 3 but sees the need to get on with it. Help from others, particularly the Leader-Developer, is essential at this stage to begin the rebuilding process.

- **Stage 5** represents the testing out of new approaches and behaviours and the inevitable learning that comes from mistakes accepted and built upon. This is the time to encourage the person to take a few risks and to test out alternatives.

- **Stage 6** is the place of completion and integration. There is a return to effective operation. Behaviours and Attitudes have shifted and integrated into a new way of life. It is significant to note that the level of competence at Stage 6 is higher than at the start of the curve, as the process of transition leads to personal growth and a better ability to cope with future change.

Attitudes to change

It is interesting to review our attitude to ourselves and others (OK Corral Model) to the Change Curve. This is particularly important when we need to deal with others experiencing change, and whose behaviours seem at odds with their 'normal' approach. By reflecting on this model, we can better assist their progress through the curve and thus help them achieve integration more readily.

At Stage 1, what often happens is that, at times, people can move from I'm not OK, You're OK to I'm not OK, You're not OK, and you need to be ready for this.

At Stage 2 it is likely that the attitude to the world, and particularly towards the perceived perpetrators of the change, will be one of I'm OK, You're not OK. People will seek to blame others and react with aggression and resistance to the situation.

By Stage 3 they are likely to have shifted and have occupied the I'm not OK, You're not OK quadrant on the OK Corral Model. They can be suspicious and hostile while harbouring all sorts of doubts and fears about their own ability to cope, and about their future and about you.

Provided they reach Stage 4 with some evidence of support around them, their attitude will once again shift. This time to one of I'm not OK, You're OK, typified by continuing self-doubts, but with a belief that others may have the answer. From the Leader-Developer's position, it is necessary to firmly demonstrate I'm OK, You're OK behaviours to prevent them from becoming Dependent and stuck in the I'm not OK, You're OK mode.

Encouragement, recognition and **confidence building** are all very helpful in assisting people to fully achieve the transition.

During this time the Leader-Developer will be on the receiving end of behaviours from the person going through the transition, some of it aggressive and hostile, at other times passive or alienated. The golden rule is for the leader to stay in the I'm OK, You're OK position, not reacting to hostility or powerlessness, but recognising where people are in the process and maintaining positive regard and support for them.

When someone is at Stage 1, they need High Support and the leader to share their vision of the desired future state, clearly and with passion. As they move to Stage 2, it is important that the leader is ready. It is dangerous for people to be in this stage of anger and denial, and they could railroad the change process by their obstructive behaviour. So this Stage requires High Challenge and High Support, repeating the vision, encouraging them through the use of appropriate rewards, setting the boundaries and going back to a much more Directing style.

Throughout Stage 3, people need High Support, recognition, encouragement and confidence building. Then, when someone starts to move from Stage 3 to 4 for example, the leader must be ready for them because, in effect, the person is holding out a hand and saying 'help'. Leaders need to spot and action this, albeit tentative, request for help, as they have earned the right to be asked by the support provided in the earlier stages. Finally, as previously mentioned, it is essential that leaders don't cause the other person to become always Dependent on them, but rather that they are enabled to become fully competent and complete the transition.

The Marathon Effect

By the time the elite runners in the London Marathon are finishing, some runners have only just started their race. They may start slowly and take lots of rests along the way. The elite runners, on the other hand, are well prepared, run at their own pace, and when they cross the line they start planning their next event. Or imagine climbing a mountain with a group. Some take off fast and reach the next base camp well before the others, but the others will make it eventually and have the motivation to reach the top.

It is easy for Leader-Developers to forget this 'marathon effect' when dealing with change. At their best, Leader-Developers will have completed their own transitions before the rest of the team gets started; they are like the elite runners or mountaineers. If you do not manage your own transition through the Transition Curve process ahead of the team, then you will hardly be in a position to support team members, whether they are 'hares' or 'tortoises'. You cannot help others unless you are in good shape yourself. You may have experienced or led change before and know what to expect; you may have, rightly, trained hard and prepared yourself so you are better positioned to cope than many of your team members.

Hopefully, you will not take on the arrogance of I+U-too often displayed by new leaders appointed to rescue or change an existing team, and who are dismissive about the difficulties some team members may have in catching up with them.

Not everyone runs or climbs at the same pace and, whether hares or tortoises, crossing the finishing line or reaching the summit and completing the transition process at the best possible speed, for them, is what matters. In this the Leader-Developer has an enormous influence, but only if they can provide the Challenge and Support needed by individuals as individuals, recognising where each person is on the Transition Curve at each step of the way, thus providing the Change Leadership necessary. To do this well requires the Leader-Developer to be well ahead in their own transition, importantly without forgetting the road they have travelled to get there.

Change and performance gain or loss

Many, if not most, step changes do not result in the effectiveness gains their organisations had envisaged. Some of this is due to the time and effort it takes to achieve effective implementation, some because the required change in behaviour never really happens, except at lip-service level.

During step change, performance parallels the Transition Curve, or Coping Cycle, as shown below. It will be noticed that it is, paradoxically at the Letting Go/Acceptance stage, where a breakthrough is poised to happen, that performance is often at its lowest ebb.

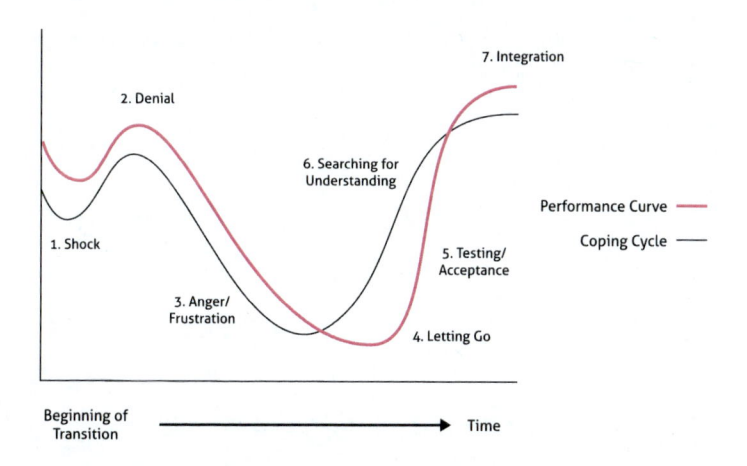

Figure: Performance Curve and Coping Cycle showing stages: 1. Shock, 2. Denial, 3. Anger/Frustration, 4. Letting Go, 5. Testing/Acceptance, 6. Searching for Understanding, 7. Integration, plotted against Time from Beginning of Transition.

The Performance Curve and the Transition/Coping one can vary along both the axes of Performance and Time. It depends, to a large measure, on the Leader-Developer, for change needs to be led and led well. It also involves developing people, as new approaches, skills and behaviours are always involved.

A situation which is not led well can result in low performance, over a long period of time, while effecting a change which is well-led will result in high performance, in a much shorter time, with much less stress for the people concerned. The potential effectiveness/

productivity gains, or losses, are significant, as is the amount of pain suffered or not. This can be shown diagrammatically, as follows:

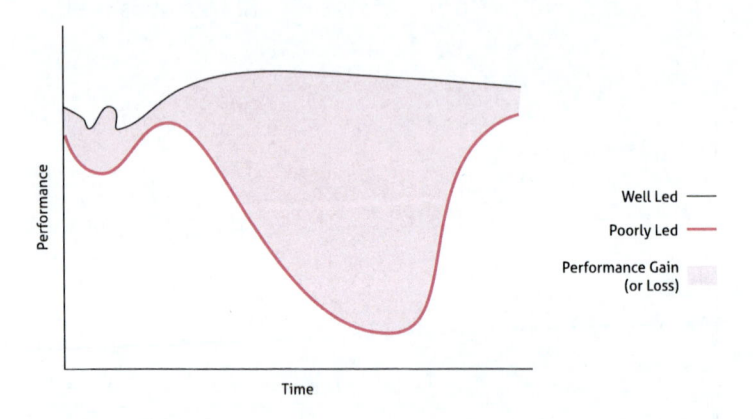

[Graph showing Performance vs Time, comparing Well Led and Poorly Led change, with Performance Gain (or Loss) shaded between curves]

What is good Change Leadership?

Good Change Leadership is simply the approach, Process and Skills we have described, applied in a particular context and in an intensive way, which places additional demands on the Leader-Developer. In many ways, it is concerned with accelerating the process, not just with the Transactional part of building people's skills, but also with the Transformational one of enabling new Attitudes and Behaviour. For most step change involves a change in the culture of 'the way things are done around here' involving a different approach to doing the job in the direction of people being more enabled and operating at a higher level of personal effectiveness.

The core of all this, and the central part of good Change Leadership, is the High Challenge-High Support approach. Again, it is both/and not either/or. Without both High Challenge and High Support, successful, enduring change is unlikely to be well implemented. Understanding the Transition Curve process will enable Support, and Challenge, to be appropriately used.

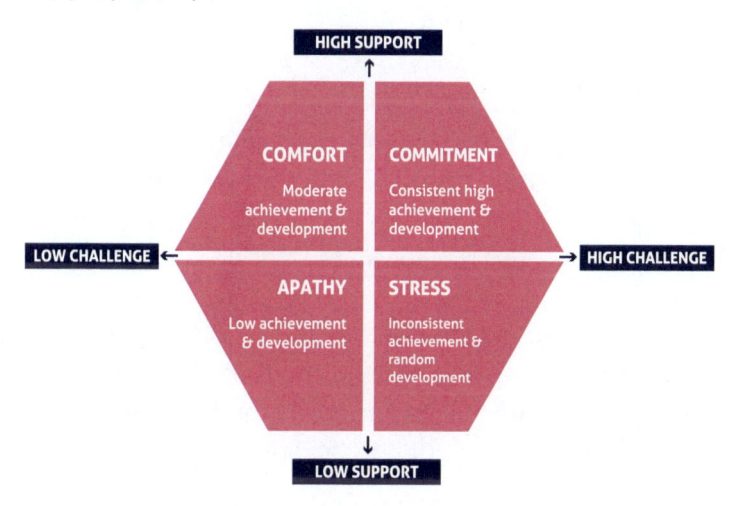

	HIGH SUPPORT	
COMFORT Moderate achievement & development	**COMMITMENT** Consistent high achievement & development	
LOW CHALLENGE ←		→ HIGH CHALLENGE
APATHY Low achievement & development	**STRESS** Inconsistent achievement & random development	
	LOW SUPPORT	

Preparing yourself to lead change

There is a saying that goes 'You cannot help others unless you are in good shape yourself'. In situations of step change, this applies particularly to the Leader-Developer. Furthermore, there is an intensity of effort required by the Leader-Developer which, unless they are in good shape, cannot be sustained. For the Leader-Developer is the role model to the team in coping with change, and what they do well, or poorly, will have an exaggerated effect.

This means that you, as the Leader-Developer, need to be through the transition process ahead of your team, or at least a stage or two ahead of them. Dealing with someone who is at the Shock or Denial stage will be much harder, for them as well as for you, if you yourself are on the 'downward slope' of anger and frustration. Letting Go/Acceptance or Testing Out is the minimum place you must be before you can start to help, rather than just colluding with others.

Be aware that you will need your own source of support – this is a reality, no matter how 'tough' you are, and if your boss doesn't provide this, you will have to find someone else you can talk things through with occasionally, outside your team.

Much will depend on whether you can commit to the new situation; if you cannot, another reality is that your working life will be frustrating and stressful, and you won't be in a position to lead or to develop.

A crucial part of this process is, again, Visioning – what will it be like when the change is implemented and working well? This will give you the future direction we talked about earlier, and also the resilience and reduction in stress which comes with goal clarity. You are also then in a position to sign on, to commit to it, or not, as well as to model what is required.

Intensity of effort

The Liberator approach is more incremental in terms of change, and when leading step change it is one of degree more than anything else. The principles and practices are the same – what varies is that step change is usually a more accelerated process, requiring a greater intensity of effort by the Leader-Developer. Additionally, the Leader-Developer has to raise their own game, to use more of the skills and principles of developing high performance, to be rock solid in leading from The Mindset of High Challenge-High Support and generally to be more active and involved. All of this needs to be done when there are likely to be greater demands on them anyway, so what is the secret?

There is no secret. We end by completing the circle. For what we have explored together is an approach and a way of life, a Process and a set of competencies that go beyond 'mere management' and which are necessary to secure your own and your team's success in today's and tomorrow's world. They are necessary anyway as part of your everyday working life and, if you apply and polish them as part of this everyday working life, you will not only harvest great benefits for you and your team, but you are also preparing yourself to cope with change.

Such step change will come and will come and come again, but like the athlete who is prepared, you will have the fitness and resources to cope with it well, while perhaps others and their teams are floundering.

This is the Challenge to you, to become a more effective Leader-Developer today, and equip yourself by absorbing the skills we have described, so that they become second nature, requiring only a touch on the accelerator when step change inevitably comes along.

So, how fit are you at present to purposefully lead change? The following checklist will give you some indication, as well as reviewing, for you, how far you have travelled on our journey together, and what you will need to do to complete that journey.

Checklist: 'How I deal with change'

The following statements relate to how you deal with change. Please indicate which answer best relates to you by ticking the appropriate box. Then consider your responses so you know where to focus additional effort.

THE TEST: LEADING CHANGE AND TRANSITION

	In managing change I...	Always	Often	Sometimes	Rarely
1	am consistent, my actions match my words and people know what I stand for				
2	talk with my people and genuinely listen to their ideas or difficulties				
3	maintain a future perspective and goal direction, not allowing myself to be swamped by confusion				
4	project a clear vision of the future to my team and transmit my enthusiasm for and commitment to it				
5	provide clarity about what needs to be done				
6	identify accurately the reasons why an individual has difficulties in coping with the change, and generate solutions				
7	make difficult/ unpopular decisions or apply strong leadership when necessary, and take ownership of the outcomes				
8	give strong feedback to help individuals achieve what is now required and reinforce progress				

THE LIBERATOR

	In managing change I...	Always	Often	Sometimes	Rarely
9	resiliently pursue my overall direction while not being thrown off course by setbacks and difficulties				
10	am highly perceptive to individual needs and motivation, and treat people as individuals				
11	flex my style appropriately to deal with varying levels of progress to what is required and a person's position on the transition curve				
12	accept mistakes will happen in trying new ways and treat such mistakes as part of the learning process				
13	actively build each team member's capability, will and confidence to deal with the change required				
14	create the situation where my team not only reach new job mastery and self-directing behaviours to meet the change successfully, but are more equipped to deal with future change				
15	always maintain strong support and encouragement to help my team meet the new challenge				

The Review: Putting It All Together

'The world is round, and the place which may seem like the end may also be only the beginning.'
— Ivy Baker Priest

Charismatic heroes need not apply! What we have described lies well within the gift of most managers. Whether you are an already established manager with many years' experience who wants to review and update your skills, or someone about to become responsible for the work of others for the first time, we wish you well.

The 'mystique' to *The Liberator* isn't a mystique at all really, but a readily understandable and accessible process. It is not to do with who you are, but what you believe in and what you do. What you believe in is central to all; it is the hub of your wheel of skills and, without this solid hub, the spokes of skills will buckle, and the wheel will not carry you and your team forward. These central beliefs, The Mindset, involve the both/and use of High Challenge-High Support, held in powerful and equal combination, underpinned by Positive

Regard and Genuineness, having high expectations and using continual, positive reinforcement.

The 4-Step Process of *The Liberator* gives a path to run on – a coherent and practical direction to follow. Within this Process there are a number of Skills, and in this book we have concentrated on the less well known or less well-practised ones, found at the Mobilising and Developing Steps of The Process.

Again, there is nothing magical about The Skills; what we have tried to do is to make them accessible to you in a digestible, usable form. We are also not advocating just one technique, for the reality is that you will be dealing with a range of people all at different stages of development and with different needs. So you must be prepared to deal with the whole A-Z, so to speak, but all with the same direction and purpose.

The purpose starts with the Underlying Attitudes and Beliefs you have, as the Leader-Developer. You start with an authentic personal style, after which you step back and watch so you can decide the right course of action before you set your clear vision.

You can then identify any team and individual changes required in explicit behavioural terms. You get to the root of issues, working out why they are occurring. With an appropriate level of assertiveness you give empowering feedback and reinforce each improvement by catching them doing it right. You understand the vital part that rewards and penalties play in the equation. You know it is a little-and-often process, but one where the need to resiliently maintain momentum is crucial, as well as maintaining your own resilience. For if you are dealing with entrenched and habituated behaviours, to make the progress you desire, you will need to work resolutely through the Mobilising Stage. It is all about a step-by-step approach.

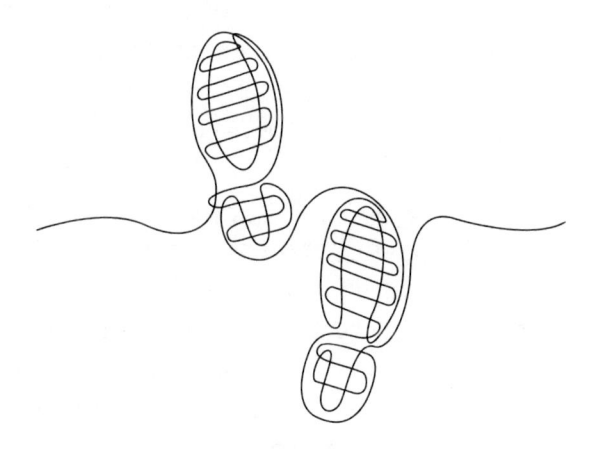

During this time, you will start to become aware of individual differences in motivation patterns, and tailor your approach to connect with individual needs, without losing sight of your Situational Consistency. Or perhaps your people are already at the stage where it is appropriate to flexibly adapt style, and you can start on the Developing and Enabling Steps of The

Process, operating more in a Transformational than a Transactional way, and encouraging Level II Learning fuelled by intrinsic motivation. Your mission is to generate continuous improvement.

Keep faith with your overall vision of enabling your people to become 'the best they can be', and for many, this will involve journeying from Dependence through to Interdependence, being self-directing in their use of Responsible Initiative, as well as having professional mastery for a particular task – that is, they can be fully empowered. You delegate task ownership and very much stay around to provide continued support. While freeing you up to do other more strategic things, you remember this is delegation, not abdication!

The same principles apply to two special applications, unlocking team potential through harnessing the power of the team, and in leading the inevitable change. Inevitable because change will always occur, it is the only certainty, and leading and developing your team in the way we have suggested will best equip them to cope well and succeed with it.

This continuous process is a voyage where you are the navigator. The continuous improvement will apply to you too. How well equipped are you for this voyage?

THE REVIEW: PUTTING IT ALL TOGETHER

The Liberator Wheel

Look at The Skills again for *The Liberator*, shown below in The Liberator Wheel. Assess where you feel you should now put your own development energies and action this – prepare yourself for the voyage.

Bon voyage!

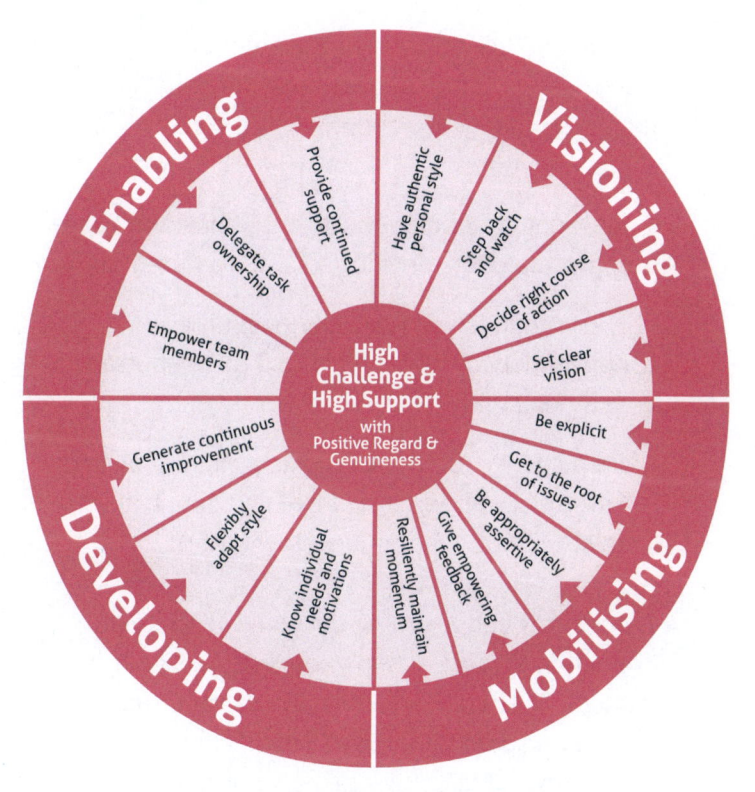

The Liberator Wheel © copyright 2023, Ali Stewart & Co and Dr Derek Biddle

293

Chapter summary

Part 1: The Test

The Liberator:

- Prepares people to deal with inevitable change, and they lead change and transition well

- Knows that continuous improvement or incremental change generally works better than step change – although when step change happens:
  - New competencies (Skills and Behaviours) have to be accepted, developed and mastered
  - Every change will have some unintended consequences which will need to be spotted and dealt with
  - Step change, often viewed as a High Challenge will, unless underpinned by High Support, lead to stress and random development

- Is ready for people going through the Change Transition Curve – when experiencing significant change. They complete this process at different rates, and some people get 'stuck' going through the curve and need practical help. Knowing which stage someone is at helps enormously in supporting that person to move on to the next stage.

- Appreciates that successful change rarely happens by itself – it is led. The leadership required demands the same Mindset, Process and Skills as those for *The Liberator*.

- Effects successful change. As Leader-Developer they are ahead of their team on the Change Curve and actively use the skills and principles of developing high performance. By completing the Change Checklist often, they hone their skills well.

Part 2: The Review

The Liberator:

- Uses the full range of Skills, being at the right stage of The 4-Step Process with each member of their team, with The Mindset of High Challenge-High Support, Positive Regard and Genuineness, I'm OK and You're OK.

- Keeps faith with their overall vision. They know it is a step-by-step, little-and-often approach to ensure the team's success, well-being, motivation and engagement and performance.

- Operates beyond mere management to inspire nations and generations to come.

Thank You

Bibliography

Alderfer, C P, *Existence, Relatedness & Growth* (New York Free Press, 1972)

Barham, K, Fraser, J and Heath, L, *Management of the Future* (Ashridge Management College, 1988)

Bass, B, *Leadership & Performance Beyond Expectations* (The Free Press, NY, 1985)

Bass, B, 'From Transactional to Transformational Leadership', *Organisational Dynamics*, 18, 3, 19-31 (1990)

Berne, E, *Games People Play* (Ballantine, 1978)

Biddle, D and Evendon, R, *Human Aspects of Management* (CIPD, 1989)

Blake, R and Mouton, J, *The New Managerial Grid* (Gulf Publishing, 1985)

Byham, W C, *Zapp! The Lightning of Empowerment* (Random House Business, 1999)

Dilts, R B, *Visioning Leadership Skills* (Meta Publications, 1986)

Handy, C, *Understanding Organizations* (Penguin, 1993)

Hersey, P, *The Situational Leader* (Warner Books, NY, 1985)

Hersey, P and Blanchard, K, *Management of Organizational Behavior* (Prentice Hall, 2007)

Hofstede, G, *Cultural Constraints in Management Theories* (University of Limburg, Maastricht, 1993)

House, R, A Theory of Charismatic Leadership, Working Paper Series 76-06 (University of Toronto, Faculty of Management Studies, 1976)

Lee, J A, *The Gold and the Garbage in Management Theories and Prescriptions* (Ohio University Press, 1980)

Maslow, A, *Motivation and Personality* (Harper & Row, 1970)

J Maxwell, *The Blacksmith* (Sphere, 1997)

McGregor, D, *The Human Side of Enterprise* (McGraw Hill, 1960)

Moss Kanter, R, *When Giants Learn to Dance* (International Thomson Business Press, 1992)

Nadler, D and Lawler, E, *Motivation: A Diagnostic Approach, Perspective on Behaviour in Organisations* (McGraw Hill, 1977)

Peters, T and Waterman, R, *In Search of Excellence* (Harper & Row, 1982)

Reddin, W F, 'The 3D Management Style Theory', *Training and Development Journal*, 21 (1967)

Schein, E H, *Organizational Culture and Leadership* (Jossey-Bass, 1988)

Schein, E H, *Career Dynamics: Matching Individual and Organizational Needs* (Addison Wesley, 1978)

Senge, P, *The Fifth Discipline* (Doubleday, NY, 1980)

Skinner, B, *Beyond Freedom and Dignity* (Hackett Publishing Company, 1971)

Stewart, I and Joines, V, *TA Today: A New Introduction to Transactional Analysis* (Lifespace Publishing, 1987)

Toffler, A, *The Third Wave* (Pan Books, 1981)

Wagner, A, *The Transactional Manager* (Prentice Hall, 1981)

Theories Explained

Theory X and Theory Y – Douglas McGregor

The background to McGregor's work was his realisation that organisations and managers within them viewed motivation from a set of assumptions about employees (what we have called here a mindset or underlying values). At that time, there were two predominant sets of assumptions. One was based on the **'scientific management' school of Frederick Taylor et al.** Here managers determined the most efficient way to perform tasks, the carrying out of which was rewarded by wage incentives. The underlying assumptions were that managers understood the work better than workers, who were essentially lazy and who could only be motivated by money. 'Thinking' (the managers) was separated from 'Doing' (the workers). This we have called the command-and-control approach, and which, in terms of human capital, neglected the view that 'with every pair of hands comes a free brain'.

Taylorism worked best where work was repetitive, and did give rise to enormous productivity gains during the era of initial mass production. However, it soon became apparent that it had many flaws, that it often reduced motivation and generated uncooperative attitudes to put it mildly, and that workers had more complex needs than those assumed.

The other was those based on the **'human relations' school of Elton Mayo et al.** The researchers found that boredom reduced motivation, that employees set group norms about the level of work they thought was right, that social contact and attention had a positive effect. Thus, instead of workers being expected to accept management's authority simply in return for wages, an emphasis was put on the acceptance of authority through treating people with consideration and allowing more participation.

McGregor identified two different sets of assumptions, positioned at the ends of a continuum that managers have about the people they manage:

1. **Theory X** – where people have an inherent dislike of work and will avoid it whenever possible, and prefer to avoid responsibility and self-direction. They can tolerate it if the pay is decent and the boss fair and considerate. Thus people must be closely supervised and controlled at work, and detailed procedures and routines established.

    Interestingly McGregor saw the human relations school as simply a more sophisticated version of Theory X.

THEORIES EXPLAINED

2. **Theory Y** – where work is as natural as play or rest, that in fact people want to work and, under the right circumstances, derive a great deal of satisfaction from it. People have the capacity to accept and even seek responsibility and self-directedness, and to apply creativity to solving problems for themselves.

Before moving on it is worth pointing out that often managers hold two models simultaneously, one for themselves (Y) and another for their subordinates!

McGregor recognised that at the time the way work was organised did not give much scope for Y, work being organised largely on a second wave basis, as described by Alvin Toffler (1981). However, it is now, through economic necessity, largely based on a third wave one, where operating in the direction of assumption Y is arguably a necessity to meet modern patterns of work and organisational survival.

First wave	Self-sufficiency	Cottage industry Craftsman approach Skilled Local focus
Second wave	Mass production	Economies of scale Specialisation/production of small parts De-skilling Hierarchical decision making
Third wave	Customer service flexibility	Decentralisation Flatter hierarchies Customer responsiveness Interdependence

Also, McGregor did not see X or Y as either/or except as a way of labelling managers' assumptions about people. In fact he subsequently argued the 'both/and' view of Theory Z, based on people being a mixture of both.

How does this fit with the underlying assumptions of High Challenge-High Support? Firstly High Challenge-Low Support can be seen as a version of X, as can Low Challenge-High Support. In its intent High Challenge-High Support fits closest with Theory Y, but–, and this is an important *but*– recognises that Z holds good in that people can be in differing starting positions or stages of development. For example, some people may have become habituated to being treated in a Theory X way, also some managers cling onto operating this way, because it is what they have learned.

In this loose sense Y is the 'meta' vision, but Z is the way it is achieved through recognising the differences in people and where they are at, working forward one step at a time. In this sense too both transactional skills are required more in the direction of X, and Transformational ones aligned more to Y.

Hierarchy of Needs – Abraham Maslow

Maslow's theory of motivation is probably the most widely known of all the motivation theories since it classifies human needs in an logical, convenient way. Although, arguably, the needs apply to the vast majority of people, they do so with different intensities and requirements. For instance one person may have a higher need for security than another and equally two people may value different ways of meeting their self-esteem needs.

Today's thinking is that for people in work, physiological needs and security needs are largely met, although there is now an argument that maintains that security is more to do with **employability** than being employed (Rosabeth Moss Kanter). This in itself has much to do with competence and being able to operate Independently and Interdependently the skills and mindset supported by the High Challenge-High Support approach.

Next in Maslow's hierarchy is the need to belong, perhaps most strongly felt outside work, but an important need inside work too. Unless people feel they are an integral part of the organisation, they are unlikely to respond to so-called higher order needs.

Maslow described two types of self-esteem needs, achievement and competence: to be good at the job and also status and recognition – achieving something important when performing the job, which has meaning. Equally for some, with self-actualisation, new responsibilities and personal growth will matter, while for others producing work of high quality will, while for yet others developing useful, creative ideas fulfils the same need. Maslow points out that individual differences are greatest at this level, which is why, if we accept that mastering performance excellence is about enabling people to operate at Maslow's self-esteem and actualising levels, a deeper and more pragmatic understanding, such as might be gained through the Motivation Inventory, about individual motivation patterns is useful.

Maslow has been criticised for seeming to suggest that his Hierarchy of Needs is applicable across all cultures. Hofstede discovered, not surprisingly, great variation among cultures, which he ascribed to differences in 'collective mental programming' based on a specific value system. For example, he found that in Sweden social needs are valued over esteem needs, while in Germany and Japan security was generally valued over social and esteem needs. In France, security needs are highly valued but so are social ones. In the UK, Canada, India and the USA of course where Maslow's work was carried out, Maslow's theory applied relatively well. Additionally there will be cultural variations within nation states, as well as between them.

Clayton Alderfer reached broadly similar views to Maslow but with some important differences in two basic ways. Firstly, Alderfer saw the hierarchy in just three categories, his ERG Theory:

- **Existence needs** – similar to Maslow's physiological needs, but extended beyond a survival level to include, for example, fringe benefits.

- **Relatedness needs** – for interpersonal relationships, similar to Maslow's belonging.

- **Growth needs** – for personal creativity and influence, again similar to Maslow's self-esteem and actualisation.

The second important difference from Maslow is that while Maslow saw people moving steadily up the Hierarchy of Needs, Alderfer argued people moved up and down the hierarchy from time to time and from situation to situation, which fits the perception and experience of many practising managers. Important in this is that if efforts to reach one level of needs are frustrated, individuals will regress (maybe in a bruised, frustrated manner) to a lower level which hits their expectations as to what is possible.

Both theories offer useful insights, but are perhaps too broad to operationalise when treating people as individuals in terms of identifying and meeting their particular differences and needs. The overall direction they are suggesting however, are very much supportive of the aims of transformational leadership and, for that matter, McGregor's Theory Y.

Two-Factor Theory of Motivation – Frederick Herzberg

Herzberg is best known for his Two-Factor Theory of Motivation, where one set of factors (dissatisfiers or hygiene factors) and the other (satisfiers), were consistently linked negatively with job satisfaction and in the case of satisfiers, positively with job satisfaction. Important in this was that high ratings for the hygiene factors did not lead to high job satisfaction, but merely to the absence of dissatisfaction – ie in themselves hygiene factors did not lead to motivation. Equally importantly, hygiene factors had to be sufficient before the motivators causing satisfaction had effect.

Hygiene factors (dissatisfiers) included such things as salary, working conditions, company policy, relationship with supervisor, while satisfiers involved such things as achievement, recognition, work itself, responsibility, advancement and growth. It will be noticed that hygiene factors are to do with the context of the job and satisfiers with the content.

Herzberg's work has been criticised for three reasons:

1. The research method – because people tend to credit themselves with their successes and blame outside factors, such as company policy, for their failures.

2. He examined only satisfaction and not productivity and its link to satisfaction.
3. Again, individual differences and needs were not taken into account.

Nevertheless, Herzberg's theory is regarded as an important contribution to understanding motivation. 'Jumping for the Jelly Beans' is a somewhat scornful description used to describe the way some managers thought extra effort could be induced by hygiene factors.

The importance of Herzberg is that, generally speaking, basic conditions (hygiene) have to be right as the starting point for motivation; they don't of themselves cause it. This fits with everyday experience where we know that such things are seen to be our 'due'. However, Alderfer has pointed out, at times of 'threat' we can alter our perspective so that security, for example, is given renewed importance. Generally though motivation comes from 'higher order' intrinsic sources, among which achievement and recognition are particularly important.

Equity Theory – John Stacey Adams

Adams' Equity Theory is to do with the ratio between an individual's job inputs and job rewards compared with the rewards others are receiving for similar job inputs. If these are not seen as fair then an individual is likely to feel aggrieved rather than motivated. The implication of this is that while allowing for individual differences (ie one person may enjoy being publicly recognised, another not), there needs to be a Situational Consistency about how people are treated.

Reinforcement Theory – B F Skinner

This is associated with B F Skinner and others, who were more concerned with the **law of effect** instead of studying inner motivation. The law of effect is the idea that behaviour with positive consequences (or good outcomes for the individual) tends to be repeated, while behaviour resulting in negative outcomes for the individual tends not to be.

This led to an approach based on behaviour modification, which uses Reinforcement Theory to change human behaviour, involving the use of **consequences** to modify a particular behaviour. There are four types:

- **Positive reinforcement** – to encourage desirable behaviour.
- **Avoidance learning** – when individuals change behaviour to avoid unpleasant consequences.
- **Extinction** – the absence of reinforcement of undesirable behaviour so that the behaviour eventually stops.

- **Punishment** – the application of negative consequences to stop or correct inappropriate behaviour.

(Note – all of this focuses on *behaviour* not *personality* and *values*, as per the Onion Model)

W C Hamner developed this into some rules for using Behaviour Modification Techniques:

1. Don't reward all individuals equally – base them on individual performance, otherwise it debases the currency and offends the Equity Principle.

2. Be aware that failure to respond can also modify behaviour – eg allowing poor performance, or not noticing good.

3. Be sure to tell individuals what they can do to get reinforcement – in other words be clear about performance standards, what is acceptable and what is not.

4. Be sure to tell individuals what they are doing wrong – don't avoid and don't confuse people.

5. Don't 'punish' in front of others – for obvious reasons.

6. Be fair – back to Equity Theory and Situational Consistency.

It will be seen that there are many connections here with what we are suggesting in what is, hopefully, a more complete approach. An illustration of this is in Chapter 3 on diagnosing performance issues where it becomes clear that it is easy to inadvertently reward the wrong thing.

Critics of Reinforcement Theory suggest that it is too simple, and for some people the idea of 'behaviour modification' is unpalatable, partly because of the view it holds of people and partly because they fear the approach can be abused. This latter is of course true, which is why it needs to be applied under a firm set of beliefs and values, such as described with the High Challenge-High Support approach (compared with, for example High Challenge-Low Support), and as a step towards the meta vision of seeing someone becoming the 'best they can be' in a context of having Positive Regard for them.

In day-to-day terms there is little doubt that reinforcement-based approaches largely work (they are used much for training). Also, in the early stages of the process, and perhaps where the leader is not yet in tune with individual needs, clear guidelines for what is acceptable and not, helps people guide their own behaviour. It is more associated with the 'push' style involved in Mobilising, and its legitimacy is in positioning the situation for Level II Learning and the 'pull' styles of Developing and Enabling. Here the issue is one of moving from getting someone to do something because you want them to do it, towards people doing something because they want to do it.

Expectancy Theory – Victor Vroom

This approach says that the effort to achieve high performance is a function of the perceived likelihood that high performance can be achieved, and will be rewarded if achieved, and that the reward will be worth the effort expended, or in other words:

- If I do this, what will be the outcome?
- Is it worth the effort?
- What are my chances of achieving an outcome which is worthwhile to me?

In all this, individual differences and needs matter greatly.

There are clear implications here for Leader-Developers, as outlined by David Nadler and Edward Lawler, which includes:

1. Determine the rewards valued by each individual – which means knowing individual needs.
2. Determine the performance you desire – and be explicit about it.
3. Make the performance level attainable – small achievable steps.

4. Link rewards to performance – associate rewards directly to the achievement, ie catch people doing something right.

5. Analyse what factors might counteract the effectiveness of the reward – clear rewards with no hidden penalties.

6. Make sure the reward is adequate – if praise is the reward, give it wholeheartedly.

Expectancy Theory overcomes to large measure the criticisms of other theories, which is that all individuals and situations are alike and that there is no one best way to motivate people. Instead it takes into account differences between individuals and situations. Its effectiveness is well supported by research and general experience, and it has wide application. It does however require managers to understand individual differences and have the perception and skill to apply it well.

There are clear links between Expectancy Theory and the process set out in *Liberating Leadership*, particularly with the Level II or Developing and Enabling part of this process.

Transformational Leadership Theory – Bernard Bass

It was Bass who first contrasted two types of leadership: transactional and transformational. As has been said, Transactional is concerned with determining what needs to be done to achieve goals, classify the requirements and get people to expend the necessary effort. Transformational leadership on the other hand, 'motivates us to achieve more than we originally expected we could', through their personal vision and energy and by connecting with our higher order needs (Maslow et al).

Bass argues that Transactional Leadership is helpful and useful, but up to a point. However, to be fully effective, particularly in today's organisational world, more is needed and that is where Transformational Leadership is required. In our language it is the difference between push and pull, between Visioning-Mobilising and Developing-Enabling.

Pat Williams-Boyd refined Bass' Transformational Leadership Theory in terms of 'new' leadership skills required. According to Boyd these are:

- Anticipating skills – in a constantly changing situation
- Visioning – including the use of persuasion and example
- Relating – being in touch with individuals' needs and motivations
- Empowerment skills – involving the willingness to share power and to do so effectively

- Self-understanding skills and frameworks – within which leaders understand both their own needs and goals and those of other people

It will be noticed that there is much linkage here between the competencies we have described in the Transformational phase of *Liberating Leadership*. Further Boyd argues strongly that leaders are 'made', through training – ie the skills needed are identifiable although complex, and amenable to training, and it is not just a case of being 'born' with them.

Robert J House makes much the same point as Bass and Boyd, but talks of 'charismatic leadership'. He describes it as 'communicating a vision or higher level ('transcendent') goal which captures the commitment and energy of people'. Such leaders centre on an 'image' of what is success and competence, and exemplify in their own behaviour the values that they espouse. They also communicate high expectations and confidence that people will perform up to those expectations.

It is perhaps a pity that this is labelled by House as 'charismatic leadership', with the grandiosity this implies and its distance from the way most managers would see themselves and their capabilities. It is basically the Transformational stage of *Liberating Leadership*, and again performance can be enhanced through training and understanding, but House neglects the Mobilising or Transactional stage, and on that basis alone it cannot be said to be complete.

There is also, in all this, one other crucial point. This is to do with the *type* of vision leaders aspire to, whether they are called Transformational, charismatic or whatever. Some such leaders have achieved much good, others much tragedy; having and bringing about a vision does not of itself guarantee that the vision is a legitimate one. This is why, as well as the practical reasons which give it effect, *Liberating Leadership* is firmly anchored in a value set which emphasises Challenge and Support, Positive Regard and Genuineness, and with a meta vision of helping people to become the best they can be in terms of their capability.

Situational Leadership Theory – Paul Hersey and Ken Blanchard

This is one of the best known of the contingency models of leadership. The term contingency describes the view that the approach that will best contribute to the achievement of goals might vary in different types of situations or circumstances – in other words 'horses for courses'.

In essence the argument is that leaders should adjust their leadership style to meet a team member's evolving desire for achievement, ability and willingness to accept responsibility – the Can Do and Will Do factors we have described. The Hersey & Blanchard model is a four-stage one, as follows, and it will be noticed that the two axes of the model are Task Behaviour

(Providing Guidance) and Relationship Behaviour (Providing Supportive Behaviour):

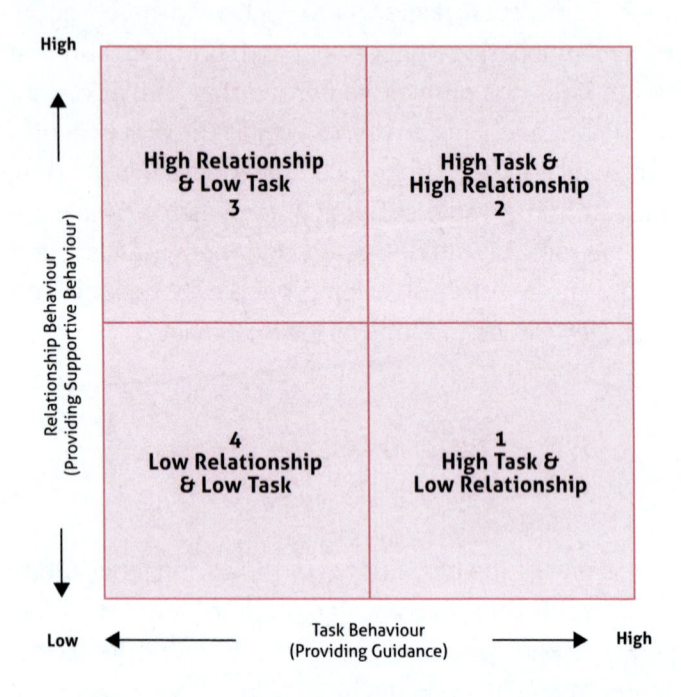

	Task Behaviour (Providing Guidance)	
High Relationship & Low Task 3		**High Task & High Relationship** 2
Low Relationship & Low Task 4		**High Task & Low Relationship** 1

Y-axis: Relationship Behaviour (Providing Supportive Behaviour) — Low to High
X-axis: Task Behaviour (Providing Guidance) — Low to High

The Situational Leadership Theory has received much interest because it describes a leadership approach which is dynamic and flexible rather than static. The motivation, experience and ability of team members must be constantly assessed to see what style is appropriate under changing circumstances. If the style is appropriate then, according to Hersey and Blanchard, it will not only motivate employees but help move them towards the next stage of development. Thus, the manager who wants to develop people, increase their confidence and help them learn will have to shift style constantly.

The main differences between the Hersey and Blanchard model and the way we have chosen to develop it concerns the underlying value set of High Challenge-High Support, with its attendant behaviours of Positive Regard, Genuineness, et al. It is firstly one of intensity of commitment for *The Liberator*, secondly, and importantly, support is there throughout, it is expressed in different ways according to the stage of development of the individual. At its extreme level at 1 (Hersey & Blanchard), it could be seen as High Challenge-Low Support (ie Low Relationship) and level 4 as the same. In level 4 they are not 'on their own' even if a task is fully delegated to them and the amount of support and encouragement is still present though different in kind.

There are too some practical issues about Situational Leadership, largely concerned with whether managers can flex their style to deal with differing situations, or whether it is better, for example as argued by F E Fiedler, to recognise that this is difficult to do and to appoint managers to fit particular situations. Experience in the UK suggests that the preferred styles are two and three, but equally the experience is that most managers are capable, through training, to increase their style flexibility.

Organisational culture – Edgar Schein

Organisational culture is a strong force, perhaps often the most important one, in shaping how an organisation actually works, performs and behaves. What it is, is a set of important understandings members share, such as norms, attitudes, values and beliefs. Schein defines it as 'The way things are done around here'.

In many ways culture can be compared with an iceberg in that while certain aspects of the organisation – eg its structure, policies and procedures are readily visible, what is less visible, and perhaps of greater mass below the surface, is the way things are really done around here. Clearly strategy and culture need to be aligned for full organisational effectiveness, which is why in recent years, when market conditions have required a change in strategy – eg customer responsiveness – organisations have paid attention to modifying their culture to support the strategy.

Part of this has been the realisation that in a fast-moving world, organisations cannot legislate and prescribe everything their employees should do to cope with new circumstances. This is why there is an increasing emphasis on values as the guiding principles on which to act. The direction of cultural change in many organisations has been towards encouraging Interdependence rather than Dependence, and 'empowerment' rather than prescriptive direction.

One body of work had a particular impact in focusing attention on the importance of culture as a determinant of organisational success. This was Tom Peters and Robert Waterman's *In Search of Excellence*. The book described the key factor – culture – in explaining the success of some major organisations. Among the cultural factors listed were, a bias for action, being close to the customer, autonomy and entrepreneurship, productivity through people, hands-on value driven, sticking to the knitting, simple form, less staff, and being simultaneously both 'loose' and 'tight' in structuring things.

However, Peters and Waterman made the point that companies with strong cultures that are focused externally – that is centred on service to the customer – may in fact be more sensitive to environmental changes and better able to adapt quickly than companies without strong cultures. In the event, many of the companies studied encountered severe difficulties when the environment did change shortly after. This introduces two important points about culture, firstly that the cultural factors described by Peters and Waterman cannot be taken as the recipe for success for all companies at all times, but that the culture needs to fit the needs of a particular organisation. Secondly, strong cultures, though a success factor at one stage can become a liability if conditions change, and the very strength of a culture can make it more difficult to change.

How does a High Challenge-High Support culture fit with this? Basically, it is concerned with keeping people fit and capable of dealing with change, as is described in Chapter 6. The only constant is change.

Our development as people (based on Stephen R Covey)

It is useful to look at the way people develop generally and also the reasons why there is sometimes a dissonance between the way people behave inside work as opposed to in their own lives.

As a baby or child we are, of course, entirely Dependent on others to feed, clothe and nurture us. And part of growing away from this state, results in teenage rebellion where we test our own boundaries and discount what others have told us. This (with any luck!) is followed by early adulthood where we have evolved a sense of who we are and what matters to us. We also feel competent to deal with most of life and to function OK with it, although our main preoccupation is still ourselves. We see ourselves as Independent people, responsible to ourselves.

The next significant stage is into maturity, where we are no longer just Independent, making our own informed decisions and coping well, but where we have the capability to operate at another phase, co-operating well with other people from the security of our own platform of self-worth, capable of taking their needs into account and proactively managing our own environment. This is Interdependency; we make choices rather than being driven by events or conditioning. This four stage process is often described like this:

a. Dependency	Directed, nurtured and sustained by others
b. Counter-Dependency	Rebelliousness, taking irresponsible initiative, being preoccupied with self
c. Independency	Taking care of self, becoming inner-directed and self-reliant, thinking own thoughts, making own decisions
d. Interdependency	Being self-reliant, proactive and capable, but also being able to join with and share productively the resources of other people

Not all people make this journey to its full extent, of course. Some get stuck permanently in Dependency, either by choice or as coping adaptation. A few are permanently rebelling, others are self-sufficient Independents who don't make the next step, embracing the potential richness of others.

Often, as mentioned, there is a dissonance between behaviour inside work and that outside of it. Frequently, this is because of expectations, the expectation that one will be told exactly what to do and be directed, that the manager is there to take care of all needs, and anyway they are paid to do so – a view often reinforced by managers under the command-and-control system recently employed. So people get habituated to this – if that's what they want that's what they'll get – and 'jobsworth' enters the scene. Other people see themselves as pursuing meaningless, boring jobs and don't invest themselves psychologically in them. Others, by default and design, find their fulfilment outside work. What happens, too, frequently these days is that people are suddenly required to operate in an Interdependent, empowered fashion overnight. This is scary and a not uncommon response is to stay with what is familiar, particularly if you are not sure the organisation really means what it says.

These are just some of the reasons which sometimes inhibit people from operating to their full abilities. They may or may not apply to you but, once the choices are made clear, most people elect to strive towards the way of life of Interdependence.

Index

Attitude	27
Broken Record – assertion technique	173
Can't Do	132
Change Transition Curve	273
Conditional & Unconditional Positive & Negative Strokes	188
Dolphins – motivation	231
Dane Gold	182
Dependency to Interdependency Model	97
Expectations Theory	48
Extrinsic and Intrinsic Rewards	182
Fisherman Fable	130
Flight Plan Analogy	192
4-Step Process, The	67
Genuineness	53
Golden Banana Award	178
Harrison Culture Model	38
High Challenge-High Support Model	34
How I Deal with Change Checklist	286
Level I and Level II Learning	234
Liberator Wheel, The	69
McGregor Theories – X, Y and Z	301

Marathon Effect	278
Motivation Inventory Categories	224
Motivation – 'relocating library' example	213
OK Corral	56
Onion Model	117
Performance Navigator	137
Pigeon Analogy	195
Positive Regard	53
Process, The	18
Reinforcement Theory	52
Rewards – list of	181
Rights & Responsibilities	45
Situational Consistency Model	245
Skills, The	19
Transactional and Transformational Leadership	71
Won't Do	132

Other Books In The Series

The Seeker

The Seeker: A clear path to developing you and your people

Ali Stewart

Are you a business owner, leader or entrepreneur... who finds managing people your biggest headache? Or maybe managing you is your biggest challenge?

If you currently lead a team, often knowing how to motivate and engage them is really hard. Some people just don't behave as you expect, some don't work well with others, some don't like their hours or pay, some consistently miss deadlines, some cause more problems than they solve. You wonder why you bother employing people at all.

THE LIBERATOR

Or maybe you're the problem. You need to get of your own way to achieve the success you deserve, and it's hard to maintain your resilience and sense of self, when there's always so much to do.

This book is your perfect guide to managing you and your people. It will:

- Put you on a path to achieving more success and balance for you
- Provide you with a superb, proven system for leading people to success
- Free you up to be more strategic and do what you're good at
- Stop you becoming distracted and ground down by 'people' issues
- Enable you to keep people happy, productive and engaged

The Seeker is a light overview, combining Insights Discovery®, *The Pioneer* and *The Liberator*, into a clear 6-Point Plan for leaders and aspiring leaders. It includes case studies and stories.

> 'Anyone looking to combine a leadership framework with greater self-awareness should read this book.'
> – Alex Keay, Insights UK General Manager

The Pioneer

The Pioneer: A powerful blueprint for greater success in your life and career

Ali Stewart and Dr Derek Biddle

This second book in the series is based on research into what makes high fliers fly!

These high fliers are the ones who become successful very quickly while still having a great life outside work. Noticeably others who work very hard seem to struggle to accomplish the same kind of results.

The key is to understand the underlying mindset of these highly successful people, and the 6-Key Skills they employ.

Success isn't down to having a high IQ, it is more to do with high Emotional Intelligence. The 7-Key Skills include managing your workload without becoming swamped; negotiating for success; managing other people well; shaping your own environment; presenting solutions not problems; and effectively planning your own career.

This book is great if you feel that you are stuck in a rut with deadlines and opportunities being missed. You can learn how to manage your manager with ease and understand the common time wasters that will catch you out time and again.

It gives you the opportunity to review and enhance your thinking and skills, raise your game, enjoy your career and lift your performance to a whole new level.

> 'It works at all levels and helps not just individuals but organisational development as well.'
> — Sue Davie, former Chief Executive, Meningitis Now

These books are available on Amazon, Kindle and Audio.

OTHER BOOKS IN THE SERIES

Ask us for information on the supporting coaching programme, The Pioneer Programme – a 6-month programme that takes you on a journey from self-discovery to mastering The Mindset, Steps & Skills of *The Pioneer*, enabling you to achieve outstanding success and happiness in life.

www.alistewartandco.com/programmes

> 'The most difficult thing is to act, the rest is merely tenacity'.
> — Amelia Earhart

Next Steps

Ali Stewart & Co
The Liberator

The Liberator Programme is a nine-month programme helping you build the rigour and skill for you to be able to lead and inspire people, with strength, dignity and compassion.

Exceptional leadership takes courage, and it is not something that talent alone can achieve. By following the principles in *The Liberator* you develop the right methods and the right practices step-by-step. We take you far deeper than 'mere management' and delve into the High Challenge-High Support model, with the tools and support to help you achieve the perfect balance, enabling you to deliver supreme performance with more grace and ease.

THE LIBERATOR

Not only will The Liberator Programme help you develop your most authentic self as a powerful Leader-Developer, it reduces stress and burnout for all, builds motivation and engagement and delivers dramatic bottom-line results for you and your organisation.

All the information you need can be found here:

www.alistewartandco.com/programmes

Contact us for a chat:

http://alistewartandco.com/contact

Or email us here: letstalk@alistewartandco.com

The Authors

Ali Stewart

Ali is a masterful leadership coach. Also a mentor, best-selling author, Master NLP Practitioner, Fellow of the Association for Coaching, and an unmistakable force in her field.

Having already built a thriving management consultancy, Ali founded Ali Stewart & Co. in July 2004. She's been a guiding light for hundreds of leaders from a whole range of industries, helping them make their mark and become exceptional in their field. Her coaching and training of executive leaders and senior teams is described as life-changing by many.

In 2008 she founded the accrediting body for The Liberator and The Pioneer award-winning programmes, and it's been growing ever since. With over 300 practitioners accredited worldwide, Ali, together with her team, hopes to welcome even more into the fold, especially trainers, coaches, leaders and HR professionals who would like to use these models to turbocharge both their growth and that of their clients or teams.

What drives Ali? A heartfelt desire to see every leader on the planet make developing people their number one priority... and for individuals to get out of their own way and allow their natural brilliance to shine.

She lives in the South of England with her husband. They have three children, and currently three grandchildren and two cats. She has a passion for music, baking and family.

Derek Biddle PhD

Initially training as a Chartered Engineer and while working at a paper mill in New Zealand, Derek became increasingly interested in the human aspect of the process. And so his study of people began.

On his return to the UK, he then trained as a Chartered Occupational Psychologist and HR Professional, assuming many senior leadership positions in major organisations, including Roffey Park Management College.

THE AUTHORS

With Ali, Derek founded Stratagem Human Resources in 1992, working with many significant organisations, including the Foreign & Commonwealth Office, Friends Provident (now Friends Life), Sunseeker, South West Water, Severn Trent Water and General Motors. It was in these organisations, and many more like them, where *The Liberator* process was distilled, tested and refined, with great success.

Derek's early training as an engineer, combined with his sound academic rigour, gives this leadership approach a distinct and logical structure, turning what many view as 'soft skills' into a process. This makes it accessible to leaders in professions who traditionally see leadership training as too fluffy.

Derek helped Ali establish the accreditation programme for coaches, trainers and consultants, before fully retiring in about 2007. As a seasoned sailor, Derek enjoys being out on his boat, and he has taught himself to play the banjo.